JOHN TOBLER

Beaufort Books, Inc.
New York

Published by arrangement with Plexus Publishing Limited, London.

Library of Congress Cataloging in Publication Data

Tobler, John
The Buddy Holly story.

Discography: p.
1. Holly, Buddy, 1936–1959. 2. Rock musicians – – United States – – Biography I. Title
ML 420. H595T6 1983 784.5′4′00924 [B] 83-17260
ISBN 0-8253-0166-1

Edited by Nicky Hayden
Designed by Chris Lower

The two films stills on the front cover are from the movie *The Buddy Holly Story*.

Published in the United States by Beaufort Books, Inc., New York.

Manufactured in Great Britain

First American Edition

10 9 8 7 6 5 4 3 2 1

Contents

Buddy Holly

'February made me shiver,
With every paper I'd deliver,
Bad news on the doorstep,
I couldn't take one more step.
I can't remember if I cried
When I read about his widowed bride,
But something touched me deep inside—
The day the music died.'
Don McLean: *American Pie*

Don McLean has never spelled out exactly what was meant by the words of his most celebrated song. But it is obvious that these lines from *American Pie* refer to February 3rd, 1959, when a charter plane travelling from Mason City, Iowa, and heading for Fargo, North Dakota, took off in a slight snowstorm, crashing on farmland only ten miles away. Its four occupants were killed—pilot Roger Peterson and his three celebrity passengers, J.P. Richardson ('The Big Bopper'), Ritchie Valens and Buddy Holly. The major casualty was Buddy Holly. He was only 22 years old, recently married, and in three years as a recording artist, had recorded a legacy of songs which has steadily grown in stature during the twenty years since his death, making him one of the genuine legends of popular music.

It is difficult to gauge the significance of artists in any field—someone who seems to be destined for megafame when he or she first appears, very often fades with the passing of time. A striking example of this phenomenon is the Beatles, whose entries in history books seemed assured on the strength of their enormous achievements during the sixties. But ask a kid now who was too young to have lived through Merseymania who were the members of the Beatles, and they are as likely to suggest Mick Jagger or Rod Stewart as Paul McCartney or John Lennon. Ask that same kid about Buddy Holly, and he will probably be able to reel off a list of famous Holly hits. Buddy Holly's songs, those that he wrote as well as those with which he was primarily associated, continue to make an impact on the top twenty on both sides of the Atlantic. Linda Ronstadt, the queen of California, has maintained and even enhanced her success by careful retreading of Holly songs, scoring top ten hits in America with numbers like *That'll Be The Day* and *It's So Easy*. In Britain in 1978, with the country still reeling from a general rejection of current musical values, Leo Sayer, a consistent hitmaker who successfully transcended the New Wave of music, rushed up the charts with *Raining In My Heart*, while even a pseudo punk, the exotically named Wreckless Eric, has turned to a Holly song in an endeavour to score his first hit in *Crying, Waiting, Hoping*. And only twenty years posthumously has the time been deemed right to produce a feature film based on Buddy Holly's distressingly short life, a film which has received unanimous critical acclaim at a time when most films based on popular music subjects are being quite rightly dismissed as extravagant folly.

American Pie poetically eulogised Holly's impact on popular music, while putting into words the unspoken sentiments of an entire generation. There can be no greater tribute to a performer from the field of rock 'n' roll music than the fact that he is still remembered with affection twenty years after his death, by millions of people throughout the world. Buddy Holly lives.

The Early Days 1936-1956

CHAPTER ONE

Charles Hardin Holley was born in Lubbock, Texas, on September 7th, 1936, the youngest of four children born to Lawrence and Ella Holley. Lawrence Holley was very much a jack of all trades—at various times, he had been cook, carpenter, tailor and all-round handyman, and it was this adaptability which had led him to Lubbock originally. Lubbock, shortly after the First World War, had become the centre of a booming cotton industry, and where a growing industry exists, there will always be a need for subsidiary services such as Mr Holley could provide.

Lubbock is hardly an entertainment mecca; even nowadays it is fairly difficult to buy an alcoholic drink in the centre of the city (full prohibition lasted until 1972) and there are reportedly more churches in Lubbock than in almost any similarly populated place in the world. Even so, that population has expanded from a few men and dogs at the start of this century to an estimated 150,000 by the 1970s, although the major industry remains agricultural. Lubbock's major advantage lies in its geographical position—on the west side of Texas, close to the border with New Mexico. However unpromising it may seem to outsiders, Lubbock's special position as the biggest centre in the south west, nearly three hundred miles from the nearest settlement of comparable size, gives its inhabitants a particular civic pride. It may seem insular to outsiders, but then Lubbock is a bit like an island in the sea of the south-west plains.

Despite the fact that Buddy Holly was born there, Lubbock is not noted for a special musical heritage—the only other currently notable musician to have connections with Lubbock is the country music troubadour Joe Ely, who went to school in Lubbock during his teenage years, and says of Lubbock, 'There was nothing to do there except sit around and play music.' Lubbock tends to import its diversions from outside, with a wide variety of visiting performers from all fields of entertainment, many of international standing. The indigenous country music, especially in the fifties, was definitely looked down upon as a 'poor relation' and, until the recent wider acceptance of country music through the pop success of such artists as Dolly Parton and Kenny Rogers, even rock concerts received a better press than country in Lubbock.

Little Charles Holley had been named after his grandfathers, but having made that filial gesture, his parents decided that to call their son Charles was rather too formal for everyday use, and following a trend which was apparently popular in Texas between the wars, they nicknamed him Buddy. That name stuck until the end of the boy's life, the only subsequent reference to Charles Hardin being in the songwriting credits of a couple of his songs, when it was politic to conceal his real identity from a previous publishing company. The 'e' in Holley was lost after Buddy's surname was mis-spelt on his first recording contract, although the family retain the original spelling.

Buddy Holly was surrounded by music in his family, although none were professional musicians. But in the south-west in the post-war years, there was a big emphasis on home-made live music and the line between professional and amateur was a thin one. The music-making Holleys were probably

Far left: One of the first publicity photographs of Buddy Holly. Buddy led the conventional existence of a small-town boy; below left: as a six-year-old fulfilling typical cowboy fantasies; and as a three-year-old celebrating Marla Kay Fortenberry's birthday party.

Buddy Holly's birthplace, 1911 6th Street, Lubbock.

like others in Lubbock who took a pride in achieving near-professional results in an acknowledged competitive situation. Keeping up with the Jones' did not just mean owning a bigger car, it meant being able to pick a guitar or tickle the ivories with more virtuosity than any of your neighbours. Ella Holley and her daughter Patricia enjoyed harmony singing, while Buddy's older brothers, Lawrence (Larry) and Travis, taught themselves the basics of guitar and piano, as a result of which Buddy first tasted fame at the age of five. Larry and Travis had entered a talent competition, and Mr and Mrs Holley persuaded them to allow Buddy onstage with them to sing a song which he had learnt from his mother. The diminutive Buddy climbed on stage and performed the number carrying a toy violin, and for his trouble was awarded a special prize, a feat which his brothers unfortunately failed to equal. But that was just about the sum total of Buddy Holly's musical aspirations until the age of eleven.

Buddy's childhood was fairly routine. The family was not particularly well-off, living in rented accommodation. 'I guess we were poor', Mrs Holley asserted, 'but of course we didn't *know* we were poor'. Inevitably, the family spoiled little Buddy as he was the youngest of four—and his mother certainly had a lasting influence on him. He could even be wilful sometimes, although this did not manifest itself until his teens, when he began to take music seriously. Prior to that he kept out of trouble while pursuing his own interests, which he seemed to keep very much to himself.

Although Buddy was reportedly very near-sighted, he was not unenthusiastic about sports, although no doubt his poor eyesight prevented him taking part in contact sports. Later on, he was said to enjoy swimming and water-skiing, but during the early years of his life, the biggest impression made on Buddy was by the church. Lubbock's high number of churches per head of population is no accident. As a local cynic put it, Lubbock is the buckle on the south-west American bible belt. The Holleys were members of a non-conformist sect, the Fundamentalist Baptists, who basically believe everything that is written in the Bible is the literal Word of God. The Church is still very much part of the social calendar to the surviving members of the Holley family. In terms of Buddy's musical development, it is interesting that the hymns sung in the Holleys' church are far closer to popular music than to the solemn dirges of much episcopalian sacred music.

It was Mrs Holley who finally decided that Buddy at the age of eleven should start to learn a musical instrument as his brothers had done. The piano was selected, not the violin, as legend had it for some years; a legend probably begun by Buddy himself for some early publicity handout. Mrs Holley's formative influence can again be seen: 'Larry and Travis already played a couple of instruments and I thought it was about time Buddy learned to play something too.' The initiative to learn the piano did not come from Buddy himself—later developments make it clear that he would probably have preferred to start straight in on the guitar but he acquiesced dutifully. 'He was kind of quiet then,' said Mrs Holley, 'Mostly kept his thoughts to himself.' Buddy was instructed by a local teacher, who reported after a few months that, despite the boy's previous lack of experience, he was a good pupil, and was able to pick up and play tunes by ear. However, after less than a year at the keyboard, Buddy's noticeable sense of urgency and desire to progress led him to move on to another instrument, which turned out to be the steel guitar. This phase lasted an even shorter time, and he moved on to the acoustic guitar. This was probably prompted by a natural desire to emulate his elder brothers, and it was Travis who taught Buddy his first few chords. After that, Buddy's natural ability took over, and within a short time, he was able to play along with the music which he heard on the radio.

'He took lessons on the piano for a while. He did very well with this and could play almost anything he wanted to—by ear.'

Until he was about thirteen, the guitar seems to have been an amusement to Buddy Holly, an amusement without any direction. But during the last months of 1949, he became friendly with Bob Montgomery at Hutchinson Junior High School. Bob shared his ability on the guitar and was able to influence Holly's musical tastes via the country music which could be heard on the radio in Lubbock. Lubbock's position made it possible to hear both country music from the Grand Ole Opry in Nash-

Buddy during his Junior High School days at Hutchinson where he met Bob Montgomery.

Above: Lubbock High School where Buddy was educated. Inset: Hank Williams, a profound influence on Holly; Williams remained the most significant performer in country music until his death aged 29 in 1953.

ville, Tennessee, about eight hundred miles to the east, and the slightly more rhythmic fare provided by the Louisiana Hayride in Shreveport, Louisiana, five hundred miles to the south-east. This was before rock'n'roll music exploded on the world, and the staple country diet was exemplified by the traditional bluegrass sounds of Bill Monroe and the tear-jerking ballads of Eddy Arnold, although one of the most popular performers of the era, Hank Williams, belonged in neither camp, and was pioneering a new form of music where lyrical content was much more personal and rhythms more deliberate. Indeed, at thirteen, Buddy's favourite song was a Williams composition, *Lovesick Blues*. Unlike places like Memphis, Tennessee, which produced a number of early rock'n'roll stars like Elvis Presley, Carl Perkins and Jerry Lee Lewis, there was little black music available in Lubbock itself, although it was possible to experiment with the radio dial and hear the blues as sung by Muddy Waters and Howlin' Wolf. The possibilities suggested of black music did not become apparent to Buddy Holly until he saw the effect it was having on musicians he admired. Tommy Allsup, a member of Holly's backing group at the time of his death, later asserted that Holly 'hated niggers', although this did not close his mind to the influences of black music.

So Buddy and Bob began to practise together, their material tending towards the bluegrass end of the country spectrum, where the majority of musicians both sing and play together rather than merely providing a backing for a main singer. Had no other interests intervened, it is not impossible to imagine Buddy and Bob treading the same close harmony path as the Everly Brothers.

Although still school boys, Buddy and Bob took the opportunity to play their music for anyone who would listen—being paid for playing was not too important in those days, although there were occasional opportunities to play at the opening of a new shop, when a musical act might help to swell the crowds. But the big opportunity came when a Lubbock radio station introduced a programme called 'The Sunday Party,' which would feature local country music talent. Buddy and Bob applied to play on the programme, and their talent was so evident that they were given a regular radio spot on Sunday afternoon. The local talent-spotting D.J. 'Hipockets' Duncan had recognised that as well as promise the boys, especially Buddy, had drive, a determination to 'get out and get going' which singled them out from among the other local hopefuls. This encouraged them to recruit a bass player, Larry Welborn, and as a trio, the group began to widen their musical repertoire. While Bob Montgomery took the solo vocal parts with Buddy harmonizing the choruses, Buddy was beginning to be influenced by the rhythm and blues he heard on the radio, and the boys began to include them in their sets. On these songs, Buddy would sing lead.

One of his favourites was apparently *Work With Me Annie,* a fairly explicit, sexy song recorded by the Midnighters on the Federal label. Holly may have sung it without realizing that the Midnighters were a black group.

Music became Buddy Holly's main interest in life, and to a certain extent, his school studies suffered. His parents were probably anxious about this. He was now attending Lubbock High School and Mrs Holley recalled that when they pulled him up about it, he would promise to bring books home, but somehow never did. In order to placate his parents, he enrolled for school courses in printing and draughtsmanship, and belonged to several school societies.

'He was a quiet kid—wasn't any great student, but didn't cause any trouble either, you understand.'

He was not, however, a brilliant student, and seems to have left no great impression on his teachers either as a genius or a dunce. After his death one of his teachers recalled that it was only after the news of the crash that he remembered Buddy had been in his class: 'He was a quiet kid—wasn't any great student, but didn't cause any trouble either, you understand.' Indeed, at this stage, Buddy seems to have done little that might seriously jeopardise his total absorption in music. Many of his spare hours during his teens were spent in the company of a steady girlfriend exotically named Echo, whom he dated for around two years until 1955 when she left to go to college, but overall little else seemed to matter other than music, which he had decided by that time was going to be his career. Bob Montgomery has confirmed this about himself as well as Buddy: 'We never really considered anything else.' There was only one, predictable, diversion and that was cars. Bob and Buddy spent quite a lot of their spare time 'cruising' round Lubbock, and Buddy was often caught for speeding, even losing his licence for a time.

A measure of Buddy's devotion to music in preference to all else was that he even refused to watch television, unlike almost all of his contemporaries, to the point where the only TV show his parents can recall him watching in those days was a Presley appearance on the Ed Sullivan Show. There were times when he would go rabbit hunting or fishing with his brothers or play games, but the majority of time was spent in the company of other music fanatics, and although Buddy played at times in jam sessions with other local musicians, his main concern was the Buddy, Bob and Larry Trio. In 1954, they tried to get themselves a recording contract, although in retrospect there was little chance that they would succeed. The mechanics of getting a record deal have changed little from that time to this, with the rider that things are a bit more sophisticated and devious today. Even so, the bread and butter method of attracting a record company is to establish a good reputation as a live act, and then to invite a record company talent scout to see you

Below left: An extract from the Lubbock High School Westerner Year Book 1954-55. Below right: Buddy was vice-president of the Vocational Industrial Club.

VIC of ICT Attends District Convention

Nineteen different trades are engaged in by the 36 members of Vocational Industrial Club of Industrial Co-operative Training, Chapter 95. These students work afternoons and have a business meeting once a week.

Socials included a formal initiation at K. N. Clapp Party House and an Employer-Employee Banquet. Tuesday nights the group played basketball or volleyball in the boys' gym.

Representatives went to a district meet in Amarillo and the state meet at Waco. Lawana Hilburn attended these as club sweetheart.

Members are Delton Combs, Buddy Holly, Charlene Hadaway, James Hogan, Bob Montgomery, Don Adams, Sarah Adams, J. C. Alexander, Don Allen, David Bowers, Carolyn Cone, Lawrence Dale, Aubrey Davis, James Fread, Reagan Garrett, Eugene Green, Billy Henson, Lawana Hilburn.

Amos Hodge, Henry Housour, George Jones, John Jackson, Wayne Jacobs, Don Ledwig, Bobby Mayfield, Jimmie Oglesby, Beverly Patrick, John A. Petty, James Pritchard, Mary Robertson, Norman Williamson, Frank Wilson, Herbert Wilson, Harold Womack, Eddie Yuzbick, and Ray Nall.

THE
RHYTHM AND BLUES
SONGSTERS OF
"SHAKE, RATTLE, AND
ROLL" FAME
BILL HALEY
AND HIS COMETS
FRIDAY
OCTOBER 14th
8:00 P.M.
FAIR PARK
COLISEUM
EIGHT STRAIGHT
RECORDING HITS
INCLUDING
"Shake, Rattle and
"Rock Around the
"Dim, Dim The
PLUS
BIG
ROCK AND ROLL SHOW

perform. This method still applies in large centres like New York, London, or Los Angeles, which are at the hub of the record industry, but places off the beaten track like Lubbock would rarely warrant a visit from a record company representative. Thus hopefuls have to turn to the less ideal, more expensive method of buying time in a recording studio to make tapes of their performances which can then be sent to record companies. This method is sometimes little more use to an out-of-town act than a live performance, when it is difficult to get record companies even to open the envelope containing the tape, let alone to play it. By submitting a tape, an act enters a lottery in which the chances of success are at best slim.

However, Buddy, Bob and Larry either did not know this or could see no other quick route to fame, and during 1954, they travelled the two hundred or so miles to Wichita Falls, where there was a small recording facility known as the Nesman Studio. Here they laid down a number of tapes, probably in several sessions, as well as using studios in Lubbock itself (at a radio station) and at Dallas. The product of one of these early sessions was given to a local radio promotion man from Columbia Records (CBS), who promised to 'see what he could do with them', but they were apparently never heard of again. So the only thing left was to continue playing live wherever there was a gig to be had, while at the same time trying to widen their sphere of operations by playing in different cities within a larger radius of Lubbock. The trio, helped out by other friends from Lubbock, continued to record whenever they could afford the time and money, sometimes even recording in their own homes on domestic equipment, and subsequent to Holly's death, a number of these recordings have been released to satisfy the enormous demand which has existed for anything at all by Buddy Holly. Buddy's role in these early recordings was still subordinate to Bob. The songs recorded were mainly country orientated without any acknowledgement to rock'n'roll, and the featured vocals are mainly by Montgomery with Buddy coming in to harmonize with his partner. Furthermore, most of the songs were written by Bob Montgomery; at this time Buddy does not seem to have shown any ambition as a songwriter himself.

With the passing of time, it has become difficult to establish exactly who participated as musicians in these sessions. Certainly, Buddy and Bob Montgomery were present, although at times little audible evidence of Holly can be detected, as his guiter playing was not distinctive in those days. On bass, it seems likely that both Larry Welborn and another Lubbock bass player, Don Guess, were used on the recordings, while the man who was regarded as the best guitar player in the area, Sonny Curtis, also helped out, sometimes playing violin as well as

Left: Buddy, Larry Welborn and Bob Montgomery at the KDAV radio station, Lubbock, 1955. Inset: An advertisement from the Lubbock Avalanche Journal, October 14th, 1955. When Bill Haley (centre) appeared at the Fair Park Coliseum, Buddy was at the bottom of the bill.

guitar. Buddy had made contact with Sonny Curtis on the 'Sunday Party' radio show and his guitar style owes much to Curtis. Don Guess had been a musical companion on and off since junior high school. No drummer was used at this time.

Nine songs remain from these sessions, and all but one were written or co-written by Montgomery. They are not notable for anything other than the fact that they mark the first known recordings of Buddy Holly. The problem with the majority revolves around their almost total lack of lyrical inspiration—no less than four of the nine include the words 'my heart' in their titles. The most interesting of these is *Flower Of My Heart*—co-written by Montgomery and Don Guess—the song was chosen for inclusion in the High School Year Book for 1954 of the school which Buddy and Bob attended. Of the other tracks, *You And I Are Through* is musically reminiscent of a bluegrass standard titled *Salty Dog,* while *Got To Get You Near Me Blues* demonstrates the limited rock'n'roll influence which Montgomery's songs would admit, although perhaps Holly's more open attitude to music, as demonstrated in his guitar break, made a significant contribution to the relative success of the recording.

One song recorded at this time, *Baby It's Love,* was co-written by Montgomery and Buddy's mother, possessing a liveliness noticeably lacking in most of Montgomery's solo compositions. This is the first concrete demonstration of Mrs Holley's gradual change from uncertainty to actual involvement in Buddy's musical career. By 1954 it was obvious that Buddy could not be diverted from his chosen direction, so it was obviously a question for his parents of 'if you can't beat him, join him'; from now on they gave him nothing but encouragement. Mrs Holley recalls late night 'jam sessions' when she and Buddy would talk about things over peanut butter sandwiches, and Buddy's associates are unanimous in their praise of the support his parents always gave him.

It was around 1954 that Buddy began to be attracted to rock'n'roll. Elvis Presley was just beginning to turn a lot of heads, although many of those heads belonged to self-styled arbiters of public morality who objected to the exciting sexuality of Presley's stage performances. But a number of other heads were turned not by Elvis's pelvic gyrations, but because his music was more exciting than anything they had ever heard before, and Buddy Holly's was one of them. He like many others made the connection between the blues he had heard played by southern black musicians and the music Presley played—if you speeded up the blues and emphasised a strong back beat, it became rock'n' roll. Three of the early Buddy and Bob recordings show the dawning of this rock'n'roll influence, featuring Buddy as lead vocalist. Elvis first came to Lubbock's Cotton Club in early 1955, and Buddy and Bob played with him the next day at the opening of a new Pontiac showroom. From then on Buddy idolised Elvis, and he tried to include Presley numbers in all the group's sets.

The strength of Elvis' influence can be gauged by Buddy and Bob's use of a drummer. Jerry Allison became friendly with Buddy and joined the group for Elvis numbers based on recordings they had heard. But as he recalls when Elvis came to Lubbock he did not bring a drummer: 'So the group went back to be just Buddy and Bob with Larry playing bass—Buddy didn't want drums 'cos Elvis didn't

Though Buddy (below) imitated the wildly popular Elvis (above), his manner was very different from the King's.

have drums.' But when Elvis appeared again at Lubbock a few months later he had a drummer in the band, and Jerry Allison was duly re-incorporated into the Holly-Montgomery combination!

Oddly enough, Buddy Holly's apparent discovery that he was at heart a rock'n'roller rather than a country singer was not strongly reflected in his first formal recording sessions. While making the informal recordings with Bob Montgomery, the Buddy, Bob and Larry Trio continued to work on stage, and their eventual big break did not occur at a gig miles away, but at a concert at home in Lubbock on October 14th, 1955. The star attractions were the rock'n' rollers Bill Haley and his Comets, who were already veterans of the recording studio, having cut their first single, *Rock This Joint,* in 1951. Around the time of their Lubbock appearance at the Fair Park Coliseum, Haley and his group were enjoying their first bout of both fame and notoriety with *Rock Around The Clock,* which is reputed to have sold more than twenty million copies since its original appearance over the credits of the film *Blackboard Jungle.* Once again, at the bottom of the Lubbock bill were Buddy, Bob and Larry, and their appearance impressed Eddie Crandall, the booking agent of the show. He signed them again for another show two weeks later, and stated his intention of trying to help Buddy Holly acquire a recording contract. It was local D.J. Dave Stone who had pointed out Buddy and Bob to Eddie Crandall and persuaded him to try and further the boys' career. Back in Nashville, Crandall wrote encouragingly that he was confident he could get Buddy Holly a recording contract, especially as Marty Robbins, whom Crandall managed, thought Buddy had 'what it takes'.

The first record company approached was Columbia (CBS), who turned down the offer, perhaps warned off by the description of the trio's act as 'Western and Bop', an epithet designed by Buddy and Bob to demonstrate their versatility. Columbia were slow in catching on to the new craze of rock'n' roll, and RCA, who were next approached, already had their token rocker in Elvis Presley, who had just been signed from Sun Records. The third company approached, Decca (now MCA), had Bill Haley on their books, but even at that relatively early stage, Haley was hardly a slim teenage idol figure, while Buddy Holly, fairly tall at five feet eleven inches and weighing just over ten stone, might have passed as a heart throb at a distance. But he was less impressive at close quarters, so it is difficult to be sure of Decca's motives in signing Holly—perhaps the most plausible explanation is that the company were signing anyone they felt might be capable of a hit record or two, rather than concentrating on a single artist, and this theory is supported by the fact that a few months after signing Holly, the company

Below: The telegram from Eddie Crandall in Nashville which led to the first recordings. Inset: Buddy and Bob's first attempt at publicity.

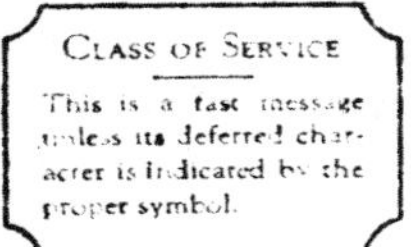

CLASS OF SERVICE
This is a fast message unless its deferred character is indicated by the proper symbol.

WESTERN UNION
TELEGRAM
W. P. MARSHALL, PRESIDENT

SYMBOLS
DL=Day Letter
NL=Night Letter
LT=International Letter Telegram

1201

The filing time shown in the date line on domestic telegrams is STANDARD TIME at point of origin. Time of receipt is STANDARD TIME at point of destination

DA011 CTA043
CT NHA035 N= PD=NASHVILLE TENN 2=
DAVE STONE=
RADIO STATION KDAV LUBBOCK TEX=
HAVE BUDDY HOLLY CUT 4 ORIGINAL SONGS ON ASCETATE DONT CHANGE HIS STYLE AT ALL. GET THESE TO ME SOON AS POSSIBLE AIR MAIL SPECIAL=
EDDIE CRANDALL 319 7 AVE NORTH=

THE COMPANY WILL APPRECIATE SUGGESTIONS

BUDDY HOLLEY
LARRY WELBORN
BOB MONTGOMERY

Buddy and Bob
"WESTERN AND BOP"

KDAV BOX 1319
LUBBOCK, TEXAS

BUS. MANAGER
HI POCKETS DUNCAN

50 **NEW PERSONALITY RECORDS • 29M SERIES**
(Continued)

78 rpm Record No.			33⅓ rpm Long Play	45 rpm Record No.
29843	The End of a Love Affair—Voc. / Love Me as Though There Were No Tomorrow	Dick Kaliman		9-29843
29844	I'm a Fool—Vocal / City of Strangers—Vocal	Tommy Smith / Tommy Smith		9-29844
29846 •	The Way You Love Me—Vocal / Similau—Vocal / Recorded by Deutsche Grammophon — Polydor Series	Caterina Valente / Caterina Valente	(A)DL 8203	9-29846 •
29847	Her First Corsage—Inst. / The World in My Corner—Inst. with Piano Solo	V. Young Singing Strings		9-29847
29848	Lonely Lover's Rhapsody—FT / The Donkey Serenade—FT	Joe Maize Orch.		9-29848
29849 •	China-Boogie—Violin Solo / Bells and Little Bells (Glocke und Glockchen) / Recorded by Deutsche Grammophon — Polydor Series	Helmut Zacharias		9-29849 •
29850	In a Little Spanish Town—Vocal with Inst. Acc. / Ol' Man River	Bing Crosby & Buddy Cole Trio		9-29850
29851	Caravan—Organ Solo with Rhythm / Avalon—Organ Solo with Rhythm	Lenny Dee / Lenny Dee	DL 8165	9-29851 / ED 2267
29852	Who Will Buy the Wine?—Vocal / I Saw Her First—Vocal	Billy Mize / Billy Mize		9-29852
29853	Dream of You—Vocal / In a Mellow Tone—Vocal	Mills Brothers / Mills Brothers		9-29853
29854	Love Me—Vocal / Blue Days — Black Nights—Voc.	Buddy Holly / Buddy Holly		9-29854
29855	Midnight in Paris / The Conqueror—Vocal with Chorus	Frank Verna		9-29855
29856	(You Gotta Get) A Lot of Livin' out-a Life / Kiss and Run—Vocal	Jeri Southern		9-29856
29857	My Wild Irish Rose—FT with Trumpet Solo / Washington and Lee Swing—FT	Muggsy Spanier Jazz Band	DL 5552	9-29857 / ED-697
29858	Darlin' (Come Back to Me)—Vocal / Another Woman's Man—Vocal	Mimi Roman / Mimi Roman		9-29858
29859	The Sand Dance—Rhumba VC / The Doggone Blues—FT VC	Guy Lombardo Orch. / Guy Lombardo Orch.		9-29859
29860	Everything That's Made of Wood—Shuffle VC / I Gotta Move—Blues VC	Louis Jordan Orch.		9-29860
29861	Jacques D'Iraque—Voc. / Too Close for Comfort	Sammy Davis, Jr. / Sammy Davis, Jr.		9-29861
29862	Don't Touch Me—Vocal Duet / Let Me Be the First to Know	The Lovers / The Lovers		9-29862
29863	Red Light, Green Light / No Money Down—Vocal	M. Torok & Tulane Sisters / Mitchell Torok		9-29863

•Available only for U.S.A., Canada and certain additional specified territories under certain conditions

25

Above: Buddy lays down a vocal in Nashville during his unsuccessful Decca session. Left: The page from Decca's 1956 catalogue which includes Buddy's first single release.

also acquired Johnny Burnette and his Rock'n'Roll Trio, whose early records sound much like Holly's first recorded rock'n'roll attempts.

There was a major snag in the contract offered by Decca however—Bob Montgomery was not included in the offer since Decca only wanted one vocalist, and Bob was more country than rockabilly. It left Buddy with an agonising decision. Should he accept the opportunity offered to him, and run the risk of alienating his best friend, or would it be better to reject the offer in the hope that another contract could be acquired which would include Montgomery? Fortunately, Bob Montgomery supplied the answer to that dilemma without much delay, insisting that Holly take the chance that was offered.

At the same time, Larry Welborn also left the trio—he was somewhat younger than the others, and perhaps felt that to turn professional before his schooling was finished was liable to affect his career options. However, Welborn remained interested in music and formed a new group, the Four Teens, who were to reappear in Buddy Holly's story before long. Jerry Allison was also unable to be considered for the first Decca sessions, for much the same reasons as Welborn. Although he wanted to go to Nashville with Buddy, the sessions were scheduled to take place during school time, and he recalls: 'Buddy got a record contract, went to Nashville and made some records, one was released, and in no time at all, we were back playing at the roller-rink just like before.' As a result, it was necessary for Holly to recruit a new band. But he chose well-tried colleagues; with

'Buddy got a record contract, went to Nashville and made some records, one was released, and in no time at all, we were back playing the roller rink.'

the enticing carrot of a record contract to encourage them, the acquisition of Sonny Curtis on guitar and Don Guess on bass was not much of a problem.

During the last few days of January 1956, the rebuilt trio drove the several hundred miles to Nashville in a new car belonging to Buddy. Guess had to strap his full blown double bass on the back of the car, causing raised eyebrows among passers-by as they drove across four states. It was a gruelling trip all round and they eventually arrived back in Lubbock broke. When they arrived in Nashville, it was to find that there was some dispute as to whether Curtis and Guess should even be allowed to play on the sessions, since they were untried musicians from the record company's point of view. It is accepted practice in Nashville when making recordings with an unknown quantity, to provide backing by full time session players to avoid wasting precious studio time with inexperienced novices. What normally results is competent, if generally somewhat uninspired, since the musicians are probably unfamiliar with the material they are asked to play, and have often never met the artist for whom they are providing the backing before coming to the studio.

Holly demonstrated a stubborn streak, and asked that Curtis and Guess should at least be allowed to attempt their expected parts in the recording, and this was finally agreed to. However, at least two session players, an anonymous drummer and Grady Martin, a rhythm guitarist, eventually took part. Martin was brought in, despite Holly's protestations, because Buddy was not allowed to both sing and play guitar at the same time, as it was felt that to concentrate on both would inevitably result in neither being satisfactory. This occasion was one of the very few during Holly's recording career when he allowed himself to be over-ruled on a matter which concerned himself. After all, a recording contract hung in the balance, and Buddy was no doubt somewhat in awe of Owen Bradley, the producer chosen for the session. Despite Bradley's reputation as a respected Nashville producer, his competence did not extend as far as the production of rock 'n' roll records. (Bradley later confessed he was out of his depth: 'We had no real experience doing what I call rock. That was sort of a disaster, I guess.')

If Decca were hoping that Buddy Holly would emulate the success of Elvis Presley, whose first single for RCA, *Heartbreak Hotel,* had been released a few weeks before, they had not taken into account the genius of Presley's original record producer, Sam Phillips. The results of that first session in Nashville on January 26th, 1956, were fairly dismal. Four tracks were recorded that day, and the abiding impression remains that Holly was trying for most of the session to emulate Presley. Two of the songs, co-written by Buddy Holly and a girl from Lubbock named Sue Parrish, have obvious similarities to *Baby Let's Play House,* which appears to have been Holly's favourite Presley song of the time. One of the two songs, *Don't Come Back Knockin',* demonstrates the stilted feeling which Bradley was unable to remove from the recordings—prior to an instrumental break Holly can be heard exhorting his comrades to 'Really rock it this time, boys,' which they signally fail to do. The other Holly/Parrish song, *Love Me,* is slightly more successful, and was actually released as a single shortly after the sessions, although it was rated as the B-side of the record, the A-side being *Blue Days—Black Nights,* a song written by Lubbock disc jockey Ben Hall, who also ran a casual band in which both Holly and Curtis had played from time to time. Hall was also trying to copy the Presley model, it would seem, as the song bears both a lyrical and musical likeness to *Blue Moon of Kentucky,* a song which had been written and popularised originally by one of Buddy and Bob's bluegrass models, Bill Monroe, before Elvis injected it with his unique attack.

Gene Vincent, an early Buddy Holly fan.

DECCA
Singing with Instrumental Accompaniment
ROCK AROUND WITH OLLIE VEE
BUDDY HOLLY

The fourth track cut is without doubt the best to emerge from this session, and possesses an exciting quality which the other three lack. The song, *Midnight Shift,* was written by a pair of unknown songwriters, Earl Lee and Jimmie Ainsworth, who had sent the song to Owen Bradley as a demonstration tape in the hope that Bradley would be able to get it recorded. Nothing much else seems to be known about the writers, so the assumption must be made that the song belongs in that strange category of 'answer' songs, a breed which were briefly popular during the fifties. An 'answer' song was in essence an attempt to cash in on someone else's big hit—*He'll Have To Stay* was the 'answer' song to Jim Reeves' *He'll Have To Go,* and *Midnight Shift* seems to bear a similar relationship to four raunchy songs made famous by the Midnighters during 1954, including the Holly favourite, *Work With Me Annie,* plus *Sexy Ways, Annie Had A Baby* and *Annie's Aunt Fanny. Midnight Shift* continues to refer to the ubiquitous 'Annie'.

Decca released *Blue Days—Black Nights/Love Me* as a single during April 1956 in America, and three months later in Britain, but it was far from being a hit. Interestingly, Gene Vincent's first recording (and first hit) *Be-Bop-A-Lula* was cut in the same studio as the Holly session, and subsequently Vincent remembered, 'I went back to the hotel and there was this fellow sitting in the lobby, who came up to me and asked for my autograph. I asked him if I'd seen him before somewhere, and he said, "Yeah, my name's Buddy Holly". He had a record out at that time called *Blue Days—Black Nights,* which was fabulous.' In spite of the accolade of his peers, the record failed to make much impression—Buddy was probably grasping at straws when he wrote to an agent that it was 'very popular around Washington DC and through Missouri'. Even though those first tracks may have been discouraging, Holly returned to Nashville six months later for another session, this time accompanied by Curtis, Guess and drummer Jerry Allison, now free of academic commitments. The three now called themselves the Three Tunes. Again, a single day was set aside for the recordings, although on this occasion, five tracks were completed. The more obvious Presley influences seem to have been noted and rejected, the myth that sounding like Elvis would guarantee a hit having been exploded by the failure of *Blue Days—Black Nights.* However, it is possible to recognise a similarity between *I'm Changing All Those Changes,* one of the Holly originals recorded that day, and Presley's *I'm Left, You're Right, She's Gone.* But the major achievements of that session, although they were unrecognised as such at the time, were the original versions of Sonny Curtis' frantic rocker *Rock Around With Ollie Vee* and the song which would become the first hit record to feature Buddy Holly, *That'll Be The Day.*

Buddy Holly and Jerry Allison leaving for the second Nashville session in July 1956, with Bob Montgomery to see them off. Inset: The label of the single release from these sessions.

That'll Be The Day was written by Holly and Jerry Allison, although latterly Norman Petty added his name to the songwriting credits. The song was suggested by a John Wayne film, *The Searchers,* in which Wayne played a typical part. In it he constantly scoffs when he disagrees with something, 'that'll be the day!' The catch phrase made such an impact on Holly and Allison that they wrote a song around it. The boys recognised the potential of *That'll Be The Day* although Owen Bradley considered it 'The worst song he'd ever heard,' but there was a small portent of the impact it was to have on the teenage market from the studio junior who thought it was the best of the session. While this version of the song is fairly similar to the hit version, what is lacking is the brilliant guitar introduction, although the famous instrumental break of the hit not only appears on this first version from the Nashville session, but also on another track cut

‘Nashville producer Owen Bradley thought ‘That'll Be The Day' was the worst song he'd ever heard.’

the same day, *Ting-A-Ling,* a song which had been a hit for black vocal group the Clovers in 1952. The final track recorded on this occasion was arguably the lamest of the lot, a Don Guess composition titled *Girl On My Mind,* which finds Holly following another trend of that era and attempting, without much success, to sing in the exaggerated style of such stylists as Johnnie Ray or Tony Williams, lead singer of the Platters.

This second day out in Nashville was deemed even less productive than the first, as none of the tracks recorded on the second day were released until after Buddy Holly had become famous. Perhaps it was the total lack of interest shown in the second Nashville session that led Holly to decide that for his third visit, on November 15th, 1956, he would not use any of his own backing musicians. Instead, he joined the system and relied totally on support from Nashville session players, including Grady Martin again and 'Boots' Randolph on saxophone, plus a rhythm section whose names have been forgotten. Perhaps the fact that all three of the tracks recorded were written by members of Holly's group, whom he had decided not to invite to the session, indicates that recording their songs was to be some kind of compensation for the apparent snub. On this third, and as it turned out, final Decca session in Nashville, three tracks were recorded, one of them being another version of *Rock Around With Ollie Vee,* which is far more professional in approach, but as a result far less exciting than the original version of five months previously. Somewhat surprisingly, two Don Guess songs were chosen in preference to *Ollie Vee* as the two sides of the single which resulted from this session. *Modern Don Juan,* the A-side, was co-written by Guess and Jack Neil, another Lubbock musician, and probably has more

Member of Associated Press—Day and Night Leased Wire Service

LUBBOCK EVENING JOURNAL

Lubbock, Texas, Tuesday, October 23, 1956

Buddy Holly "Packs 'Em In"

Young Singer Is Lubbock's "Answer To Elvis Presley"

energy attached to it than many of the Nashville tracks, although, like the other two tracks cut at this session, it lacks the life which slight imperfections might have given it. The other track, *You Are My One Desire,* is basically a routine slow ballad. This second single, predictably, was no more successful than the first, and as a result, Decca decided during the early weeks of 1957 not to take up their option to continue making records with Buddy Holly, and after just one year as a Decca recording artist, Holly was again looking for a record deal.

These sessions amounted to a time span of nearly a year. Meanwhile, Holly and the Three Tunes continued to work live, frequently playing as opening act and even sometimes backing group for the stars who passed through Lubbock. They joined a couple of tours through the south-eastern states, but compared to the professionals they were still amateurish. 'We were a little "green",' Holly wrote. There were hard times too—Hipockets Duncan recalls getting a *cri de coeur* at the Clover Club in Amarillo: 'Hipockets,' wailed Buddy, 'we're *hungry*!' Hipockets booked them for teenage dances where they played rock 'n' roll exclusively. There was the inevitable rock 'n' roll diversion, too: Sonny Curtis recalled that in Nashville they often 'hung up at Marty Robbins' office and chased chicks'. One reason why Buddy personally was broke was revealed by his brother Larry who loaned him the money to buy a new $600 Fender Stratocaster electric guitar and amps early in 1956. Buddy's determination surprised his brother, who naturally advised caution. 'I know what I'm doing,' Buddy retorted. 'I'm going to be a star now, and everything I do has got to be the best.'

The boys also recorded a quantity of informal demos during this period, which were probably never meant to see the light of day, but after Holly's death were dusted off to supply the demand for any Holly material, no matter how dire. Not that everything recorded in this fashion was dire—at least half the nearly twenty tracks which survived need no defence in terms of performance or of quality, although much of the quality achieved was supplied by Norman Petty and the Fireballs some years after the original recordings. Eleven of the songs recorded informally were cover versions of already famous songs which had been recorded for the most part by stars of the era, and which Buddy presumably liked enough to want to incorporate them in his stage act, so the tracks give a clue as to the flavour of his live sets. They included Fats Domino's *Blue Monday,* the Presley arrangement of Roy Brown's *Good Rockin' Tonight* and Clarence 'Frogman' Henry's *Ain't Got No Home.* There was also a preponderance of Presley related material, including *Blue Suede Shoes* and *Shake, Rattle And Roll.*

A curiosity of these sessions was Bill Doggett's million selling instrumental hit, *Honky Tonk,* a favourite twelve-bar blues tune used by many guitarists to practise during the fifties, but perhaps the two most interesting tracks from these sessions were the covers of Chuck Berry's *Brown Eyed Handsome Man* and Bo Diddley's eponymous theme tune. Both became big hits in Britain when they were eventually released after 'doctoring' by Norman Petty. What is most impressive about these two tracks is that they see Buddy Holly no longer slavishly copying the original versions of the songs, but successfully arranging them in a distinctively Holly way. One recording from this time was not a rehearsal tape; *Have You Ever Been Lonely?* was a country standard, which was apparently a favourite of Mrs Holley's, and it seems that Holly's version of the song was recorded as a present for her, particularly in view of his quite audible shout of 'Mother' at the end of the track.

Above: One of Buddy's own early publicity shots.
Below: Local boy makes good.

'I know what I'm doing. I'm going to be a star now, and everything I do has got to be the best, and my guitar has got to be the best.'

Then there are the 'originals', some of which, including *Changing All Those Changes, Love Me* and *Don't Come Back Knocking,* are merely alternate takes of songs recorded in Nashville for Decca. Most of the others are fairly routine songs—both *Baby, Won't You Come Out Tonight* and *I'm Gonna Set My Foot Down* are reminiscent of early Elvis, and *I Guess I Was Just A Fool* (written by Holly) and *It's Not My Fault* (co-written by Ben Hall again, with noted Nashville pedal steel player Weldon Myrick) are fairly nondescript. *Because I Love You,* on the other hand, is one of the best of Holly's early songs, a well-written emotional ballad, while *Rock-A-Bye-Rock* is a fairly standard early attempt to write a song around the recently coined term 'rock', but again contains the guitar solo which would later emerge in *That'll Be The Day.* The final artefact from this era is another instrumental, credited, oddly enough, to Buddy's mother as composer. The song, *Holly Hop,* seems to have come from the 'fun' sessions which produced *Ain't Got No Home,* and demonstrates some of the guitar figures which would later appear on Holly's hit records.

There may, of course, be many more informal recordings from this period in existence, but so far, none have been released, and there is no concrete evidence to support the possibility. Even so, the comparatively large number of tracks which Buddy Holly laid down in one form or another during 1956 is an indication of his overwhelming desire to become a rock'n' roll star—his surviving recordings indicate a major progression from plagiarism, as demonstrated by the Presley copies, through to full-time reinterpretation, with songs like *Bo Diddley* and *Brown Eyed Handsome Man.* It would not turn out to be a long wait before Buddy Holly began to achieve his desire, but just a matter of a few months.

The First Year Of Success-1957

CHAPTER TWO

1957 saw Buddy Holly back at square one. His first experience with making records had been a failure and, perhaps as a result, the only member of the Three Tunes still interested in playing with him was Jerry Allison. Buddy's mother recalls that for many months, Jerry's drums were set up in her front room, so that he and Buddy could get on with rehearsing without the delay of setting up the drum kit. A number of the home recordings which came to light after Buddy's death were made with just Buddy and Jerry participating.

Holly had been proud of his musicians—in his first known interview in a Lubbock paper, he referred to them as 'a three piece orchestra just like Presley's', so perhaps he was a little dejected when two of the three members decided to quit. The reasons for their departure were not precisely the same. Neither had been invited to the final recording sessions with Decca, but, perhaps as compensation, the three songs recorded had been written by either Curtis or Guess. Don Guess would probably have been happy to stay (his subsequent lack of musical pedigree would indicate that the sessions in Nashville were the nearest he got to being a rock'n'roll star), but Jerry Allison is quoted as saying that his motive for leaving may have been because Holly suggested that he should buy his own double bass. In view of the lack of success the group had so far encountered, Guess was reluctant to make such an expensive investment.

Sonny Curtis' departure was also partly related to finance. As a player whose first love had been country music, he was not convinced that rock'n'roll was the coming thing; Curtis felt that he was far more likely to make a steady living out of country music. He had also noticed Holly's rapidly improving guitar technique, which had led to Holly playing lead more often than Curtis, although it had been the Curtis style which Holly had copied in their early days together. Curtis found himself out of the spotlight as a rhythm guitarist, and saw no reason why he should retreat any further towards obscurity.

Left: The Crickets in late 1957. Below: A Norman Petty publicity photo, featuring his foot! Clockwise from the top: Holly, Allison, Mauldin, Sullivan. Above: Roy Orbison, one of Norman Petty's early discoveries.

Neither Guess nor Curtis seem to have been replaced immediately, and Holly and Allison continued to rehearse and play gigs, often as a duo, but at times with other musicians joining in. This period of enforced isolation had one beneficial effect which was later to stand them in good stead. By practising and playing together so much they developed an interdependence which meant that each of them could, to a large extent, anticipate how the other would respond to a fresh piece of music. Curtis is quoted as saying of this period: 'Boy, that was some good stuff when Allison and Holly were just picking by themselves.' It also meant they could save more money for future plans.

Early in the year, Buddy Holly became aware of the NorVaJak studio in Clovis, New Mexico. This was owned by Norman Petty, his wife Vi and Jack Vaughn, the third member of the Norman Petty Trio, an 'easy listening' group who had several medium sized hits during the early 1950s. The biggest of these was their version of Duke Ellington's *Mood Indigo* in 1954, the royalties from which had allowed the trio to purchase and begin to equip their studio, originally intended only for the recording of their own releases. The existence of a well-equipped studio quickly attracted other recording artists in the vicinity. Soon Petty was working as a producer on other people's material as well as his own. The studio was unique at the time in that Petty did not charge by the hour for the use of his recording facilities but allowed his customers to continue until they felt that they had achieved a satisfactory result.

' Norman Petty saw in Buddy Holly an artist-composer with a greater future than that of any ordinary rock and roller. '

The first important rock'n'roll record to emerge from the studio was *Ooby Dooby,* which heralded the start of Roy Orbison's career. (Orbison had been encouraged to pursue it by a schoolfriend, Pat Boone.) In late 1956, a pair of even bigger hit tracks was recorded there. The Rhythm Orchids, a local group formed at school in Canyon, Texas, were receiving such great encouragement from their audiences at live concerts that they decided to make their own record. NorVaJak was the nearest studio they knew about, so the group, which had two lead singers in Buddy Knox and Jimmy Bowen, went in to record a couple of tracks, with Bowen singing lead on *I'm Stickin' With You* and Knox on *Party Doll.* Subsequently, Roulette Records in New York heard the disc, which was sent to them by Norman Petty, and the tracks were separated appearing as the A-sides of two singles which both sold a million copies. This success was achieved despite the fact that the studio was not equipped with sufficient space to allow the participating musicians to play as loud as they would have liked. Consequently the group's drummer had reluctantly been forced to abandon his newly purchased and very expensive, set of drums, and play on a cardboard box in order to avoid drowning Buddy Knox's vocals.

The Rhythm Orchids' session made Norman Petty something of a celebrity in local musical circles, as he had both produced the tracks (although the term 'producer' was generally not in common use at the time) and had also helped to get them released nationally. Buddy Holly was one of those who was impressed with Petty's prowess. Petty's association with several hit records and the fact that NorVaJak was the closest studio to Lubbock (Lubbock and Clovis are about one hundred miles apart) made the studio the logical place to record some new demo tapes. It's reported that Holly's opening gambit to Petty was along the lines of 'If you can get Buddy Knox a hit, you can get Buddy Holly a hit'. Petty was intrigued by this confident approach and asked to hear some of the songs Holly intended to record. When Holly and Allison thundered out some of their new material, Petty was sufficiently impressed to suggest that it might be better to try and assemble a full group for the recordings in order to increase their selling potential.

At this point Holly and Allison did not intend to use Petty to sell the demos as they thought they already had a contact with Roulette Records through another musician, Gary Tollett. Allison and Holly had played as backing musicians for Gary Tollett on a recording session at Clovis and in return for their assistance Tollett was going to arrange with his cousin (who worked at Roulette) to

Right: The Crickets on stage during 'The Biggest Show of Stars for '57' tour. L. to r.: Niki Sullivan, Jerry Allison, Buddy Holly, Joe Mauldin. Inset: Norman Petty on a visit to London in the early sixties.

send their tapes there. Another guitarist, Niki Sullivan, whom they met on this recording session later agreed to throw in his lot with Allison and Holly as rhythm guitarist to Holly's lead. Now all they had to find was a good bass player. Buddy contacted his old colleague Larry Welborn and this became the line up for the first formal recording sessions by Buddy Holly at Petty's studio in Clovis.

The two tracks recorded by the quartet on February 25th, 1957, were *That'll Be The Day* and *I'm Looking For Someone to Love*—backing vocals were added later, although it seems that Niki Sullivan's main role in these recordings was as a backing singer rather than as a guitarist. Even though the tracks were designed as demos, Holly was worried. Despite the fact that Decca had

Young hopefuls—the Crickets during 'The Biggest Show of Stars of '57' tour.

dropped him from their artist roster, he was still contractually forbidden to record any of the songs which he had made for Decca. *That'll Be The Day* was one of the songs to which Decca claimed ownership, so it was necessary to hide his identity within a group name before sending the demos to Roulette. The name chosen was, of course, the Crickets.

A popular fallacy surrounds the choice of name. It concerns the discovery of such an insect in the echo chamber of Norman Petty's studio, and a sound not unlike that of a cricket can be heard on *I'm Gonna Love You Too,* which was recorded by Holly at the studio a short time later. However, the truth of the matter is that in America during the fifties it was fashionable to name groups after birds or animals, well known examples of the genre being the Flamingos, the Orioles and the Penguins. Holly and Allison spent some time looking through an encyclopedia belonging to Allison's mother, and finally decided that they should call themselves the Crickets—not a bird or an animal, but the nearest thing to a singing insect. (It's no coincidence that a few years later, another quartet also investigated insects as a possible source for a group name . . . and came up with the Beatles.)

Norman Petty assisted with the production of the tracks, and it was the first occasion on which he collaborated with Buddy Holly. His impact on Holly's music has been likened to the effect George Martin had on the Beatles as a catalyst for talent which was already in existence, but which required direction: 'Right back in 1956, when I first met him, when he wandered into my studio in Clovis, New Mexico, to make a demonstration tape, I said then that he was a diamond in the rough and I was right. Although I discovered him, I let him go his own way. He knew what he wanted and I knew how to record him. He respected my ability and I respected his personality and talent. I was no magician where Buddy was concerned. You don't create talent—it's there'.

The two tracks turned out extremely well, but

before they could record further tracks the newly named Crickets had to play some live dates. Unfortunately Welborn did not have time to work live with the group, as he was playing guitar with another group called the Four Teens. One member of the Four Teens was a sixteen-year-old bass player, Joe B. Mauldin, who had known Jerry Allison at school. Mauldin, after some discussions with Holly, agreed to take Welborn's place to complete the quartet. By the time the Crickets were ready to go back to Clovis to record the two tracks which would complete their demo tape, Mauldin was a fully integrated member of the group. In fact, *Last Night,* one of the songs which was recorded during that second session, Mauldin had written himself and already performed with the Four Teens. The other song recorded on that occasion was a version of a song that would later become a hit for the Crickets, *Maybe Baby*. The

‘Although I discovered Buddy, I let him go his own way . . . I was no magician where Buddy was concerned. You don't create talent—it's there.’

song was probably conceived before Buddy Holly was fully into the swing of writing songs. His mother used to try to help him, but Holly generally considered his mother's lyrical ideas far too serious. It was after one of these ‘too serious’ judgements that Mrs Holley wrote down a few basic lyrics for *Maybe Baby*, and Buddy liked the idea so much that he completed the song.

Having completed their four-track demo tape, the Crickets asked Norman Petty to send the tape to Roulette Records for them. Roulette claimed to like the songs, but not the performances. The suggestion was made, however, that Buddy Knox should record *That'll Be The Day* and Jimmy Bowen *I'm Looking For Someone To Love.* For many young songwriters, the chance to have songs considered as follow-ups to million-selling singles would be eagerly accepted, but Buddy Holly disagreed and refused to give his permission.

Following Holly's refusal to allow Bowen and Knox to record his songs, Norman Petty offered to use his contacts with other record companies in an attempt to get the Crickets a recording contract. His first attempt, an approach to Columbia Records to whom he was personally signed as an artist, bore no fruit. The company's head of talent acquisition was one of the last record company executives to see that rock'n'roll was going to be an enduring form of music. Following that, Petty sent the tapes to a music publishing concern, Southern Music, who passed them on with a recommendation to Coral Records. Ironically, Coral was an autonomous subsidiary of Decca, the company which had dropped Holly a few months earlier from their

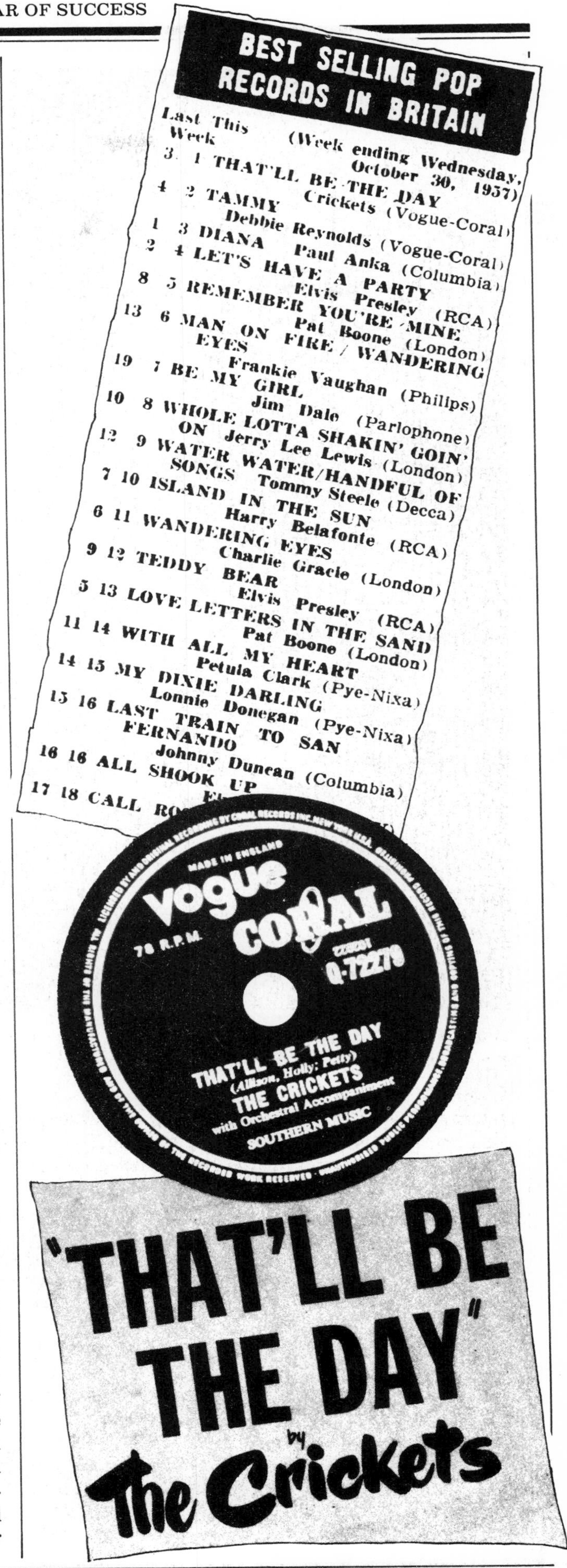

BEST SELLING POP RECORDS IN BRITAIN

(Week ending Wednesday, October 30, 1957)

Last Week	This Week	Title	Artist (Label)
3	1	THAT'LL BE THE DAY	Crickets (Vogue-Coral)
4	2	TAMMY	Debbie Reynolds (Vogue-Coral)
1	3	DIANA	Paul Anka (Columbia)
2	4	LET'S HAVE A PARTY	Elvis Presley (RCA)
8	5	REMEMBER YOU'RE MINE	Pat Boone (London)
13	6	MAN ON FIRE / WANDERING EYES	Frankie Vaughan (Philips)
19	7	BE MY GIRL	Jim Dale (Parlophone)
10	8	WHOLE LOTTA SHAKIN' GOIN' ON	Jerry Lee Lewis (London)
12	9	WATER WATER/HANDFUL OF SONGS	Tommy Steele (Decca)
7	10	ISLAND IN THE SUN	Harry Belafonte (RCA)
6	11	WANDERING EYES	Charlie Gracie (London)
9	12	TEDDY BEAR	Elvis Presley (RCA)
5	13	LOVE LETTERS IN THE SAND	Pat Boone (London)
11	14	WITH ALL MY HEART	Petula Clark (Pye-Nixa)
14	15	MY DIXIE DARLING	Lonnie Donegan (Pye-Nixa)
15	16	LAST TRAIN TO SAN FERNANDO	Johnny Duncan (Columbia)
16	16	ALL SHOOK UP	
17	18	CALL RO[illegible]	

roster, but Bob Thiele, the Coral employee who listened to the tapes, was so impressed that he prevailed upon Decca to allow him to work with the group. In the last week of May, just three months after they had made the demo tape, the Crickets found themselves with a single released which used the original demos of *That'll Be The Day* and *I'm Looking For Someone To Love.*

Almost automatically, Norman Petty took over as Buddy and the Crickets' manager. He saw in Buddy Holly a writer bubbling over with good songs, too many good songs for just one group to record. In 1957 the maximum number of singles that one artist was allowed to release in a year was usually about four. Even allowing for LPs, there were still great songs coming from Holly's pen, as well as from other local writers, which would be lost to Petty and Holly if they were not immediately recorded. So Petty conceived a scheme, for which everyone should be grateful in retrospect, which enabled the Crickets to have their singles released on the Brunswick label (another Decca subsidiary), while Buddy Holly solo records would come out on Coral.

The Crickets' *That'll Be The Day* was released in America on May 27th, 1957, and gradually climbed the charts until it reached the top twenty after three months. It eventually peaked at number three at the end of September 1957. In Britain, progress was considerably speedier. *That'll Be The Day* was released in Britain on the Coral label to an audience who had quite probably heard the record several times on Alan Freed's radio show, 'Disc Jockey Jamboree', to which thousands of amazed teenagers listened every Saturday night on Radio Luxembourg. After only three weeks it reached number one in the British charts, where it remained for three weeks during November 1957, until it was replaced by that year's Christmas hit, *Mary's Boy Child* by Harry Belafonte.

Even before *That'll Be The Day* had entered the American charts, the first Buddy Holly solo single was released, coupling another Holly original, *Words Of Love,* with a cover version of *Mailman, Bring Me No More Blues,* a song recorded by another Coral artist, Don Cornell. *Words Of Love* was an obvious classic, although it was not recognised as such at the time. It was a complete failure in America and was never released as a single in Britain, except as a posthumous B-side. Perhaps the reason for the record's failure was due in part to Holly's relative inexperience of the record industry. Having recorded the song, he had allowed it to be sent to Southern Music, who had become his music publishers, before the record was released. Perhaps not realising that Buddy Holly had expressed a very definite preference for recording his own songs before anyone else could be allowed to use them, Southern played the song to the Diamonds, a vocal group who had scored a huge hit earlier that year with *Little Darlin'.* The Diamonds, who at the time

Buddy and Joe B. Mauldin performing at the Brooklyn Paramount in September 1957.

were searching for material with hit potential, liked *Words Of Love* sufficiently to record the song and release it even before the Holly version was publicly available. Although their version was not a major hit, it made the Holly recording seem like a cover version, rather than the other way round.

It was particularly unfortunate for Holly because he had recorded the song with an ingenuity which was very new in that era. On the record, Holly sings in unison with himself. Today this is neither difficult to achieve nor particularly unusual. The miracle of the multi-track recorder has made the process fairly straightforward. This certainly was not true in 1957. Norman Petty says that he only knew of two such machines existing in America, one belonging to Atlantic Records and the other to Les Paul, the man who single-handedly pioneered the use of overdubbing. But the lack of such a facility did not deter Buddy Holly, who considered that *Words Of Love* would sound far better if the vocal parts were sung by two voices in unison, both of which should be his. The only way in which this effect could be achieved was by recording the voice and backing once, then playing the recording back through a mixing desk and adding another vocal line, all of which would be recorded on another tape machine. As Norman Petty noted later, this was not easy—the singer who was adding the additional vocal would have to remember precisely every inflection and piece of timing that he had used on the first vocal in order that the final sound should not come out as contrived. But Buddy Holly was able to achieve an identical vocal—as Norman Petty says, 'He had a unique capability, an inborn sense of timing, and *Words Of Love* sounds like two people singing the same thing at the same time'.

Although it was undoubtedly a blow to Buddy Holly at the time, the record's lack of acceptance made little difference to the excitement which had been created by the success of *That'll Be The Day*. Almost overnight, the Crickets jumped from being fairly well known in Lubbock to being big stars throughout America. On the strength of that popularity, they were booked to play on a giant, nationwide, package tour which was to play eighty dates without a break, starting on September 6th, 1957, and continuing until close to the end of the following November. This tour was not quite the first that the group had played outside a radius of three hundred miles from Lubbock. As their hit record had climbed the charts, the Crickets had played some dates on the East Coast of America, although it would seem that they might never have been booked for some of those dates if it had been known that they were a white group. When they discovered that they had the only white faces on the bill, the group must have been just as surprised as the people who had booked them. Holly may not have felt too much at ease at the start of these dates, fronting a group who had been brought up in redneck Texas, where a colour bar was still practised, and the audience reaction which the group received was at best lukewarm. That is until, as Joe Mauldin remembered, 'Buddy turned round to us and said "Let's play *Bo Diddley*".' With the audience then convinced that the Crickets could appreciate black music as much as they could, it was plain sailing.

Before they left on the tour, Holly and the Crickets laid down some new material which could be released on record while they were away. Eight Holly solo tracks and another five which would eventually be released under the name of the Crickets were recorded during the summer of 1957. Included among these thirteen tracks was some of the finest music Holly would record. Many of them

Left: The Crickets used several songs by Bo Diddley. Above: The original British sheet music for Holly's first solo hit. Right: Buddy at the New York Paramount, Christmas 1957.

were to remain unrecognised masterpieces until after his death. But three songs were hits at the time of their first release, and several more achieved fame later, both as original recordings and in cover versions by other artists.

Of the 'solo' tracks (although, of course, the backing was provided by the Crickets on these tracks), two were cover versions of hits of the time, both of which were originally recorded by black artists. *Valley Of Tears* was released by Antoine 'Fats' Domino, one of the true originators of rock'n'roll, which he started recording not long after the Second World War, long before Alan Freed invented the phrase in 1954. *Valley Of Tears* was a hit for 'Fats' during that summer of '57, so Holly probably recorded the song simply because he had heard it and liked it. *Ready Teddy* was a little different, as the song was an established favourite, having been released by both Little Richard and Elvis Presley.

'Buddy said "If you don't get it right this time, we're going to change it back to 'Cindy Lou'." But the second time we got it and it stayed 'Peggy Sue''

Most of the other 'solo' songs were credited to various combinations of Holly, Allison, Mauldin, Sullivan and Petty as songwriters, although doubt has been cast on the authenticity and accuracy of some of the credits. Buddy Holly was a prolific songwriter, although he never really explained how he went about it. His father described him as 'a peculiar-type songwriter'. He would go out for two or three hours alone in the evening. 'Then he'd come back', recalled Mr Holley, 'go straight to his room, pick up his guitar, and start to sing'. But of course the original lyrical theme and melody would then be worked over with the other Crickets who would add, subtract and refine the 'first draft', as it were. So it is small wonder there was confusion over the credits. As to Petty's involvement, it must be remembered that the Crickets at the time were young and relatively carefree, and songwriting royalties were not an item to worry over. Subsequently, of course, several of the songs in question have earned huge sums in royalties, either in their original versions or in innumerable cover versions.

Initially, the Crickets were very much an unknown quantity, while Norman Petty was a more established name, so he arranged with the group that his name should be added to the credits as extra weight. As Joe Mauldin told John Goldrosen, 'Who's to say that the disc jockeys would have played our records if Norman's name hadn't been on them?' Among the songs to which this may have applied were the two which together formed the second Buddy Holly solo release (not counting the earlier Decca material), *Peggy Sue* and *Everyday*. Coincidentally, both also profited at the time of recording from the fact that Norman Petty's studio was too small to have the facility of a separate drum booth to isolate the noisiness of the drummer, an almost standard studio feature these days. Jerry Allison was a very noisy drummer, although at the same time extremely inventive, and on *Peggy Sue*, as Norman Petty remembers, 'He had come up with a very clever and exciting beat, but he was so noisy, we couldn't hear Buddy. So we moved Jerry into the reception room with his drums and a microphone and I was able to put the drums through an echo chamber and control the volume through the various passages of the song.'

The lyrics of the song have become a bone of contention over the years—originally the song was called 'Cindy Lou', after a cousin of Buddy's who at the time was two years old. Later, Jerry Allison suggested that 'Cindy Lou' be changed to 'Peggy Sue', the name of his fiancée (now ex-wife). More recently, this same lady told *Rolling Stone* that there was never any question of the song being titled anything other than *Peggy Sue*. Whatever the truth, the record of *Peggy Sue* remains one of the finest pop singles ever made; it also became Buddy Holly's first solo hit, reaching the top ten in both Britain and America by the end of 1957.

Everyday, which was released as the B-side of

Left: One of the most familiar publicity shots of Buddy, which he apparently didn't like too much. Right: The first professional publicity picture of the Crickets.

the single, has also become a classic, and again the reasons partially concern Jerry Allison's drumming. *Everyday* is a gentle ballad, and, almost inevitably, Allison's drumming was overwhelmingly powerful. While it was being decided what should be done about it, Norman Petty heard Allison playing the pitter-pat rhythm of the song on his thighs. As he was wearing tight jeans, the sound produced seemed to fit perfectly with the requirements of the song, so Petty arranged a microphone about four inches from Allison's thighs, and the unique percussive sound of the song was captured in that way. But that was only half the innovation of the record. Petty suggested providing a tinkling backing on the celeste which greatly added to the charm of the song.

Norfolk Municipal Auditorium
AIR-CONDITIONED
Tomorrow Night--2 Big Shows 8:00-11:00 P.M.
SUPER ATTRACTIONS presents The BIGGEST Show of Stars for '57
ALL IN PERSON
Fats DOMINO and his Orchestra
Frankie LYMON
La Vern BAKER
Chuck BERRY
Clyde McPHATTER
the CRICKETS
the Spaniels
the Drifters
ALL IN PERSON
"DIANA" PAUL ANKA
JOHNNIE & JOE "OVER THE MOUNTAIN"
"Mr. LEE" the BOBBETTES
HAROLD CROMER M.C. ★ Crying TOMMY BROWN
PAUL WILLIAMS and his BIG ORCHESTRA
GET TICKETS EARLY

Whether or not the songwriting credits of *Peggy Sue* and *Everyday* are incorrect, Jerry Allison is certain that there is no truth in the assertion that Norman Petty, Joe Mauldin and Niki Sullivan wrote *I'm Gonna Love You Too* with which the record credits them. Allison contends that he wrote the middle section of the song, while Holly wrote the verses, but they are the only two people involved in it who are not credited. The record is a fine example of the lasting qualities of the songs Buddy Holly recorded. Two of the other 'solo' songs from the session have similar titles, *Listen To Me* and *Look At Me,* but are in fact very dissimilar songs, and occupy very different positions in the league table of Buddy Holly compositions. *Look At Me* is a fairly routine song on the subject of suspicions of infidelity between a boy and a girl. The vast majority of Holly's lyrics are about love and only rarely did he write a song outside the sphere. *Listen To Me,* on the other hand, is arranged in a highly ingenious manner, with the refrain being spoken rather than sung, yet another example of the invention prevalent in Norman Petty's studio during these sessions. *Listen To Me*

‘Buddy's guitar playing influenced my drumming more than anything. I haven't played with anyone since, that I could play with as well.’

enjoys a more dubious distinction—when it was released in America early in 1958, it was a complete flop, and it only stayed in the British chart for two weeks.

On a couple of the tracks recorded during this period, Vi Petty would add piano backing. But for the last of the Buddy Holly sessions recorded

Above: Clyde McPhatter and (right) Chuck Berry, two more of the artists on the bill in the 1957 package tour. Left: Tour poster from 'The Biggest Show of Stars of '57', with the Crickets some way down the bill.

during the summer of 1957, an outsider, in the shape of C.W. Kendall Junior, played piano. He also re-wrote the song *Little Baby,* sharing the songwriting credit with Holly and Petty. Not surprisingly, the tracks which were eventually released under the Crickets' banner were a similar mixture of two cover versions and three originals. Once again, Buddy Holly's admiration for the work of Little Richard is demonstrated, this time in the shape of a version of *Send Me Some Lovin'*, half of a double-sided hit for Richard during the first half of 1957, the other half being *Lucille.* The other cover version was *It's Too Late* by Chuck Willis, known as 'The Sheik of the Stroll'.

A third song from this era, *Oh Boy!,* had originally been the work of a pair of local musicians, Sunny West and Bill Tilghman, who had initially titled their song *All My Love.* Norman Petty has subsequently been quoted as saying, 'Probably the most accurate thing I've been given credit for was being a keen observer. I didn't create anything, Buddy was the creator, and I was able to capture on tape what Buddy created.' But in the case of *Oh Boy!* he and Holly together altered the lyrics of what was at best a promising song, and made it into a smash hit on both sides of the Atlantic during December 1957. It was another example of a song which would transcend the time of its first recording. The B-side was *Not Fade Away,* a curious Bo Diddley influenced staccato composition by Holly and Petty. On this song, Holly double-tracked in the same way as on *Words Of Love,* overdubbing several backing vocal lines which each used his own

'He was a different person when he was on stage. He would tear up an audience.'

voice. The final Crickets song from these sessions was *Tell Me How,* which was later destined to become merely a single B-side, although Jerry Allison remembers the song as one of his favourites of those he recorded with the Crickets.

With a store of finished recordings behind them, the Crickets were able to embark on their first big package tour with some confidence. The show was somewhat presumptuously billed as *The Biggest Show Of Stars For 1957*, but it could legitimately lay a claim to such a title. Apart from the Crickets, Fats Domino, the Everly Brothers, Frankie Lymon and the Teenagers, Paul Anka, Chuck Berry, the Drifters, Jimmy Bowen, Clyde McPhatter and Lavern Baker were on the bill. All were stars at the time, and many still enjoy that status today. The explanation for the large number of performers in a single package was quite simple. The object of 'package' tours at this time was to allow the audience to see as many acts as possible within a time scale of two to three hours. The result was that you did not see very much of anyone, but what was

Lubbock Combo On Network Show Next Sunday

Four Lubbock youths who have scored a success in the recording and personal appearance field with their music will hit the nation-wide audience on Sunday, Dec. 1, when The Crickets are slated to appear on the Ed Sullivan Show.

The boys, ranging in ages from 18 to 21, are former students of Tom S. Lubbock High School and won plaudits for their record "That'll Be the Day" and have a new tune on the rise, "Oh Boy!" and an album set for release Dec. 1, "The Chirping of the Crickets."

Completed Tour

Managed by Norman Petty, The Crickets have just completed a tour of the East and West Coasts and Canada in the show, "The Biggest Show of Stars of '57," headed by Fats Domino. They compose their own music and do their own playing without stage orchestra assistance.

The Crickets are composed of Buddy Holly, vocalist, son of Mr. and Mrs. L. O. Holly, 1305 37th St.; Jerry Allison, drummer, son of Mr. and Mrs. J. D. Allison, 2215 6th St.; Niki Sullivan, guitarist, son of Mr. and Mrs. Matt Sullivan, 3102 44th St.; and Joe B. Maldin, bass viol, son of Mr. and Mrs. W. C. Mulcahy, 2401 St

Left: Buddy during the Bell Sound Studios session. Above: The original British album sleeve for the first Crickets LP. Above right: Report from the Lubbock Avalanche Journal announcing the Crickets' appearance on the Ed Sullivan Show.

played during each act's allotment of perhaps fifteen minutes was likely to be at least familiar, and most of the time, a proven hit. However, little consideration was given to the artists, who were booked to play two shows most nights, after which they would all pile on a claustrophobic bus which would transport them several hundred miles through the night to the next venue.

Inevitably it was very difficult to sleep on a coach with thirty-odd other people, as the conditions were both uncomfortable and noisy. Apparently, Buddy Holly could often be found at the back of the bus, gambling with Chuck Berry, but the racial harmony indicated by such a scene was not always the rule. At some point, it is alleged that Lavern Baker punched Holly in the face, knocking his glasses off and pushing him into some mud, after a particularly undiplomatic remark about her colour.

This tension was probably not helped by the discovery that for certain dates on the tour, the white acts would not be able to perform, as it was illegal in certain states for black and white performers to appear on the same stage. Niki Sullivan recalled the pressures of segregated touring. Going from Atlanta, Georgia to New Orleans the tour buses were actually stopped by two patrol cars; they forced the 96 black performers into one bus and the 20 whites into the other. 'They informed us that in New Orleans there is no way that blacks and whites are going to appear on the same programme,' Sullivan said. 'The blacks were taken to one hotel, the whites were taken to another, and then we were informed we could not appear on the same show.' However, this enforced break was put to good effect by the Crickets to record the last four tracks required for their first LP.

Buddy Holly regarded the presence of Norman Petty at his recording sessions as crucial—not surprising as his involvement with the Crickets had coincided with their first hit record. It was therefore necessary to work out a mutually convenient date and location where recording of the last four tracks could be undertaken. This turned out to be an airforce base near Oklahoma City during September 1957. The Norman Petty Trio had been booked to play at the Officers' Club on the base and Petty acquired permission to use the club and brought with him the necessary recording equipment.

Buddy and the Crickets joined him, and four tracks were laid down by morning, when the group would have to rejoin the tour. 'We recorded the major soundtrack,' said Petty, 'then Buddy continued on the road and I took the tape back and added the voices and echo in New Mexico.'

The album, coyly titled *The 'Chirping' Crickets,* was released around the end of the eighty-day tour and remains one of the finest debut albums ever made. But even before it hit the shops, both Buddy Holly and the Crickets had scored top ten single hits in America with *Peggy Sue/Everyday* and *Oh*

Boy!/Not Fade Away respectively. In Britain, it was a similar story, although achieved with greater speed—*Oh Boy!* entered the British chart within a week of release, and *Peggy Sue* did not take very much longer to become the first Buddy Holly solo hit. In America, Decca attempted to cash in on Holly's new found fame by re-releasing their version of the song.

In December 1957, the Crickets, riding high with several hits, made their first nationally networked television appearance on the *Ed Sullivan Show.* They played *That'll Be The Day* and *Peggy Sue.* Between the two songs, Sullivan spoke with Buddy briefly, but it was fairly obvious that the name of Buddy Holly meant nothing to him and that he did not altogether approve of their music. Holly was nevertheless polite, a constant feature of the very few interviews he did which have survived.

It seems that there were two Buddy Hollys. One was at heart a country boy, who helped his father and brothers equip Norman Petty's new echo chamber with the ceramic tiles which were part of the family business, and who put up with dumb questions from uninterested interviewers who considered themselves more important than the people they interviewed. This same country boy was also reflected in the clothes which Buddy and the Crickets wore. When they started playing professionally on the eighty-day tour, it was T-shirts and jeans, but by the time the group went to New York for the Ed Sullivan show, the Everly Brothers, with whom the Crickets had struck up a good relationship, suggested that suits would be more elegant. From that time on, Holly never appeared on stage looking less than smart.

This demonstrated the other side of Buddy Holly—as Jerry Allison puts it, 'He was really confident, more interested in music than anything else, and quite convinced that he was going to make it as a recording star.' This confidence did not prevent Holly from listening to advice that was offered, although as Hipockets Duncan noticed, his mind was often somewhere else at the same time: 'He was always in a hurry, trying to do so much, and his mind would be working on more than one thing at a time.' Off-stage Holly was a quiet, likeable person but when he stepped on-stage, Norman Petty remembers him as 'Much more extrovert—when he was performing, he was an uninhibited genius'. But it wasn't entirely spontaneous. His wife Maria later claimed that he always thought out his performances ahead of time, planning them in detail with Jerry and Joe.

Then there was the question of Holly's spectacles. At the start of his career, Holly wore rather unattractive metal framed glasses, but again around the time of the New York visit at the end of 1957, it was suggested to him that if he was going to wear glasses, he might as well make it obvious, and get a pair that could become a trade-mark. The result was the black-rimmed glasses which he wears in most of the better-known photographs. As Elton John remembered, 'I'd started wearing glasses to hide behind. I didn't really need them, but when Buddy Holly came along, I wanted a pair like his! I began to wear them all the time, and as a result, my eyesight got worse!' Another trademark was Holly's guitar—at the time of the Nashville sessions, he had played a Gibson acoustic, much like most of the other musicians around, but when the Crickets were first formed he brought his new Fender Stratocaster, which was something of a novelty in those days.

At the end of 1957, a lot was happening for the Crickets on the positive side. But not everything was positive—after the long tour, Niki Sullivan decided that he had had enough of being a Cricket,

Left: Buddy wasn't averse to using a capo on his guitar for fast key changes. Below: The Everly Brothers.

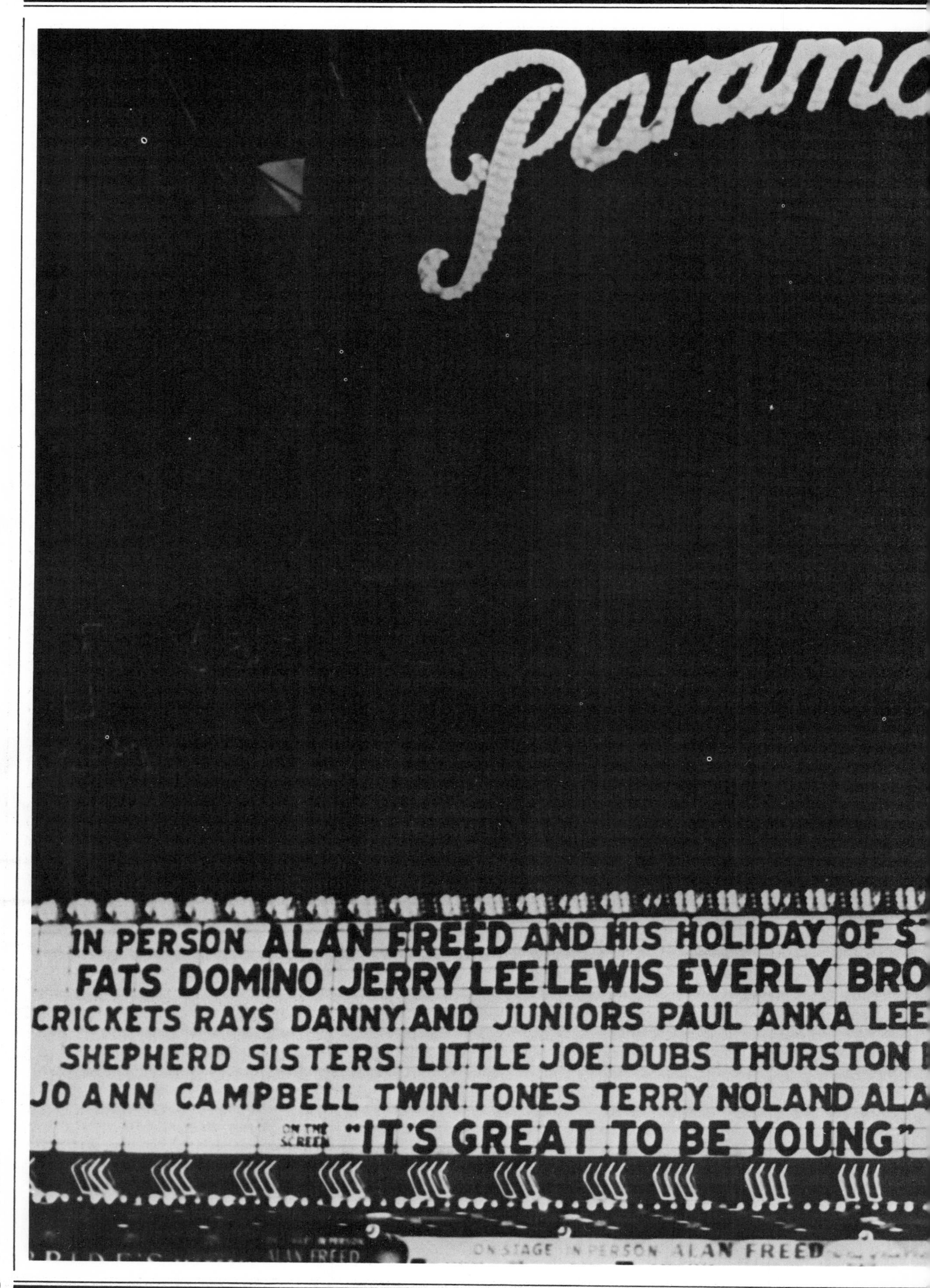
IN PERSON ALAN FREED AND HIS HOLIDAY OF
FATS DOMINO JERRY LEE LEWIS EVERLY
CRICKETS RAYS DANNY AND JUNIORS PAUL ANKA
SHEPHERD SISTERS LITTLE JOE DUBS THURSTON
JO ANN CAMPBELL TWIN TONES TERRY NOLAND
ON THE SCREEN "IT'S GREAT TO BE YOUNG"
ON STAGE IN PERSON ALAN FREED

and left the group. He was not a native Texan like the other three—according to the sleeve note on *The 'Chirping' Crickets*, he was born in Southgate, California, although he had moved to Texas at an early age. This may have led Sullivan to feel something of an outsider, added to which he was not a close friend of any of the other members of the group. But these may have been minor items compared with the fact that he was constantly in the background, playing second fiddle to Buddy Holly, although he too wrote songs, played guitar and sang. Once again Holly's guitar playing had improved to the point where there was usually no need for Sullivan to participate in recording sessions. However, Sullivan did leave one almost indelible mark on rock'n'roll history—the sleeve of *The 'Chirping' Crickets* shows Jerry Allison with a somewhat oriental look, which was due to Sullivan

'When we played the New York Paramount we did better than anyone else on the whole show.'

punching him in the eye during an argument a little while before the photograph was taken.

The Crickets briefly toyed with the idea of inviting Sonny Curtis to join them as Sullivan's replacement, but Curtis was not interested, as he was on the verge of acquiring his own record contract, and anyway, was not about to put himself back in the position from which he had escaped a year earlier. So the group decided to continue as a trio. Their first bookings in this form came in the shape of something similar to the mammoth package tour which they had finished only a few weeks previously, in that a large number of acts were on the bill. But there was also a major, and pleasant, difference on this occasion. The shows were all to take place at the same venue, the Paramount Theatre in New York, which meant that all the travelling which had been so debilitating on the eighty-day tour was absent. The show played for twelve days over the Christmas period with another magnificent bill, including Fats Domino, Jerry Lee Lewis, the Everly Brothers, Buddy and the Crickets, the Rays, Danny and the Juniors, Paul Anka, the Teenagers (but this time without Frankie Lymon, who had left the group to go solo), half a dozen other acts of lesser note, and the whole lot introduced by Alan Freed, the prime rock'n'roll disc jockey. It must have been an incredible show, although, by the end of the twelve days, the participants may not have been looking their best. Each act had to perform up to six times per day, before retiring to a convenient hotel. Nevertheless, it was an excellent manner for Buddy Holly and the Crickets to end a highly successful year.

Left: The front of house display for Alan Freed's Christmas show at the Paramount Theatre in New York.

The Year Of Peggy Sue-1958

CHAPTER THREE

1957 had been a year when all Buddy Holly's frustrated ambitions had been realised. But his continuing desire to progress would only allow him to stop working when he and the other two Crickets would see their friends and family on brief visits to Lubbock. During one of these trips home, the group had time to record another song, *You're So Square,* which had been previously sung by Elvis Presley in the film *Jailhouse Rock.* Elvis had sung the song under its proper title of *Baby I Don't Care.* No doubt the reason for this being recorded was that once again record company pressure to finish twelve tracks suitable for an album had left Holly with insufficient material of his own. *Peggy Sue* held the number three position in the American chart at the start of 1958, and the time was perfect for a Buddy Holly solo album.

Not that there was much time for anything other than performing during January 1958. After their brief lay-off over the New Year period, the group went back on the road. This time the tour was for only three weeks and culminated in their second, and final appearance on the Ed Sullivan Show in New York towards the end of January. Due to the fact that Holly and Sullivan apparently did not particularly like each other, the Crickets were relegated to the final minutes of the show. This only gave them enough time to play *Oh Boy!,* a song to which Sullivan had objected during rehearsal, presumably on the grounds that it was not in keeping with the 'family viewing' aspect of his show. Subsequently, Holly refused to appear on the show again, despite a considerably increased financial offer, doubtless feeling that the Sullivan show was not worth the trouble involved.

However, that stopover in New York was used to advantage in two other ways. Holly, having already brightened his image with smarter clothes and new glasses, took the time to have his teeth capped. Although appearance was important, the Crickets realized that their appeal was not as 'teen idols' like Eddie Cochran or the Everly Brothers, but as musicians. Jerry Allison said, 'Compared to Frankie Avalon and all those slick dudes, we were just a bunch of ugly pickers who just picked. But really, that made it all seem better.' The stopover also took the Crickets into a recording studio in New York, Buddy's first experience of a major studio since the Nashville sessions. Two tracks were recorded, again to try to complete Holly's first solo album, but only one was considered a success at the time. *Rave On,* written by Sunny West, Bill Tilghman and Norman Petty. The song is generally considered to be one of Holly's finest recordings, as he transforms what might have been a fairly routine number into an exciting *tour de force.* Regrettably, the other track cut, *That's My Desire,* was a comparative disaster. The song had been originally recorded in 1947 by Frankie Laine, and seems totally unsuitable for the Crickets. The version has never been released in America to this day, although in Britain it did come out in 1971 as part of an album of oddments entitled *Remember.*

At the start of February 1958, the Crickets embarked on their first overseas tour, which was to take them first to Australia—with a stopover in Honolulu on the way—and later to Britain. In Australia, everything so far released, with the

Below: The Crickets began 1958 with a smart new image. Below right: The logo for the group's first tour of 1958.

exception of *Words Of Love*, had been a big hit. On the tour, the Crickets were accompanied by another young prodigy from America, Paul Anka, who, although only sixteen years old at the time, had achieved a massive hit with his second single *Diana*. The record stuck at number two in the American charts, but was number one for nine weeks during the summer of the previous year in Britain. So Anka was big business, as was the other American artist on the tour, Jerry Lee Lewis, whose *Great Balls Of Fire* was a worldwide smash hit at the time. The Americans were supported on the bill by a top Australian favourite, Johnny O'Keefe, and the tour was a great success. This is particularly remarkable as it seems to have been the first antipodean tour by any American rock'n'roll stars.

After a brief return to Lubbock and a short tour of Florida, the trio were off again to Britain, where their reception was equally enthusiastic, although the four week tour began and ended with some minor disasters. On the second day, the Crickets appeared on the *Sunday Night at the London Palladium* television show and, due to a combination of nerves and technical problems, were not at their best. Just before their last appearance, Joe Mauldin knocked off the caps on Holly's front teeth whilst fooling around in the dressing room, and Holly had to go on stage with chewing gum smoothed over his teeth. The incident unnerved the group and Norman Petty told them later that it was the worst show he had ever seen them do.

The rest of the tour was a great success, however, and helped increase the Crickets' record sales in the U.K. It was a very tight schedule, taking the group on a wide-ranging series of one-night stands round England, from Southampton to Blackburn, from Newcastle to Bristol. It was a new experience for Buddy Holly and the Crickets, touring as the only rock'n'roll group in a Variety Show replete with juggler, lady ballad singer and comedian—in fact Holly wrote to his parents that his jokes were getting bigger laughs than the comedian—in this case Des O'Connor. The group therefore had to appeal to a far greater range of tastes than they were used to, but soon got into the swing of it, attracting rave reviews from the music press.

'Who knows, we might change and become comedians instead of rock and roll stars.'

'Fierce, blistering, exciting—and authentic!' enthused one critic. 'This was the real, genuine, finished article.' From the *New Musical Express'* description of the Crickets' 'tremendous, belting, twenty-five minute act' full of 'enthusiasm, drive and down-to-earth abandon', we can begin to appreciate the raw energy of a live Holly session. Even the unfavourable reports in the national press, which was in the midst of a rock'n'roll backlash at the time, give us a tantalising glimpse of Holly's frenetic stage style, described by one

Buddy relaxing in Hawaii, where the Crickets played a successful date in January 1958, en route to Australia (below right).

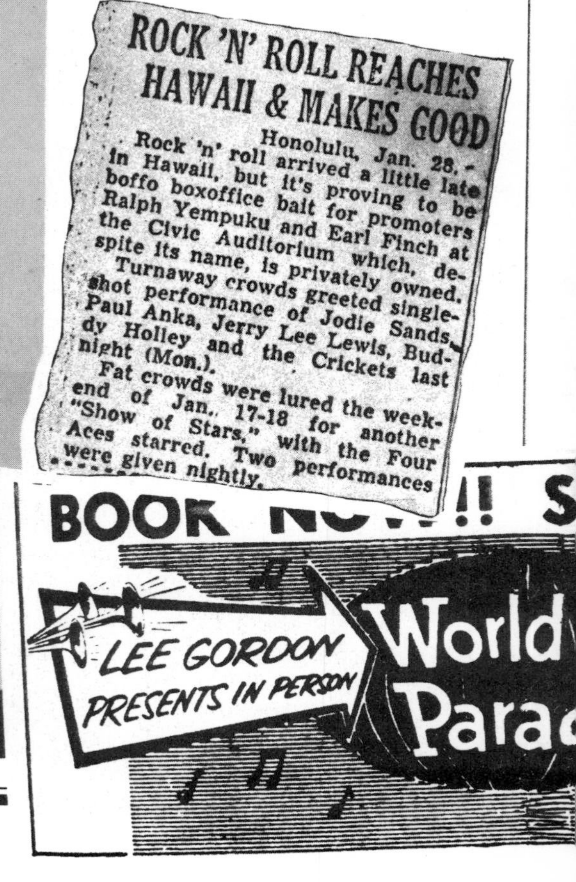

ROCK 'N' ROLL REACHES HAWAII & MAKES GOOD

Honolulu, Jan. 28. - Rock 'n' roll arrived a little late in Hawaii, but it's proving to be boffo boxoffice bait for promoters Ralph Yempuku and Earl Finch at the Civic Auditorium which, despite its name, is privately owned.

Turnaway crowds greeted single-shot performance of Jodie Sands, Paul Anka, Jerry Lee Lewis, Buddy Holley and the Crickets last night (Mon.).

Fat crowds were lured the weekend of Jan. 17-18 for another "Show of Stars," with the Four Aces starred. Two performances were given nightly.

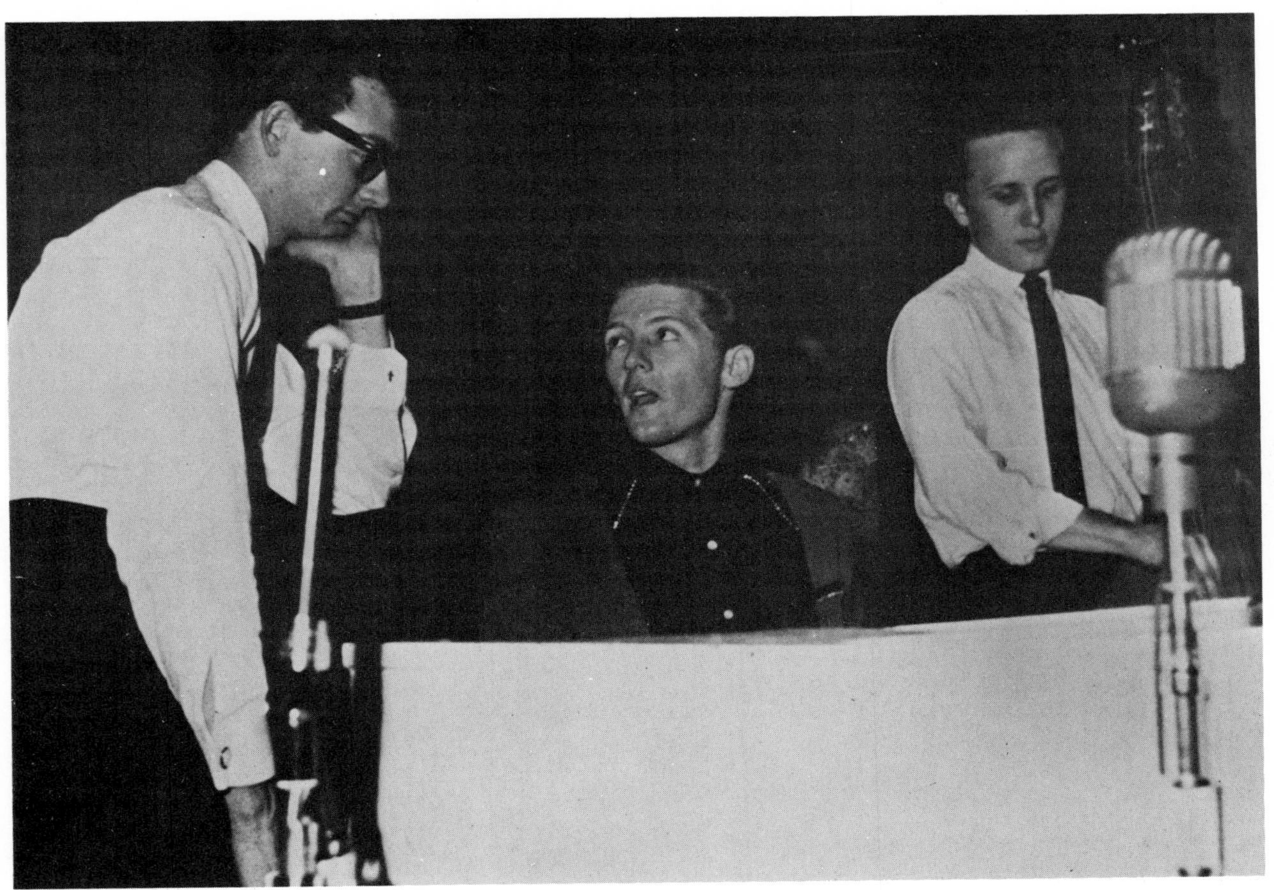

Buddy Holly and Joe Mauldin rehearsing with Jerry Lee Lewis (centre) during the Australian tour.

reporter as 'foot-stamping' and 'knee-falling'. The same reporter wails: 'Where on earth is show-business heading?' Two days after Buddy Holly and the Crickets returned to the States, a segment they had taped for BBC TV's *Off the Record* was shown, providing them this time with more successful television exposure. The group had enjoyed their stay in England, but were relieved to be returning home, away from the chilly English spring weather.

Melody Maker, however, Britain's top music paper, was not completely sold on the Crickets' performance, noting that when Holly 'added the Presley movements, he seems so obviously out of his depth', but British fans were unmoved by such criticism, and continued to purchase both Buddy Holly and Crickets records in vast quantities. While their American counterparts virtually ignored the Holly single *I'm Gonna Love You Too/Listen To Me,* and only allowed *Maybe Baby/Tell Me How* into the top twenty for two weeks, in Britain both records came into the charts within a few days of release, with the Holly record reaching number sixteen and *Maybe Baby* number four. The first trips outside America were both highly successful.

Back in the U.S.A., the Crickets set off on yet another national package tour, again under the leadership of Alan Freed and accompanied by a star cast including Jerry Lee Lewis, Chuck Berry, Larry Williams and the now solo Frankie Lymon. It was while they were on this tour that the first Holly solo album, simply titled *Buddy Holly,* was released. The strangest feature of the album is its sleeve picture of Holly, which features him without glasses. This may have been taken during a brief experimental period when Holly tried to wear

Above: Buddy with the Tanner Sisters, who supported him on his British tour in 1958. Right: The Crickets, wrapped up against the unfamiliar British weather.

contact lenses and sometimes even went on stage without any form of visual assistance. As John Beecher points out in the sleeve note to a reissue of the album during the seventies, 'Only after he had dropped his guitar pick and been unable to find it, did he wear glasses on stage'. The photo session which produced the sleeve picture may easily have been the last time that the 'public' Buddy Holly appeared without glasses, and it shows all the characteristic awkwardness of one who is pictured without a familiar accoutrement. Nevertheless, *Buddy Holly* remains an excellent album, if not quite the equal of *The 'Chirping' Crickets*—many of the tracks would be hit singles in their own right sooner or later, and the album demonstrates Holly at his most inventive.

Despite all the success they had achieved in three continents, Holly was still eager that the Crickets should continue to work, and in a brief between-tours rest, the group returned to Clovis to cut four more tracks, two of which would eventually be Crickets' sides and two released as solo items. The first one of these to appear on record was *Take Your Time,* which became the B-side of the single release of *Rave On.* The song was a collaboration between Petty and Holly, and is particularly memorable for its organ part played either by Norman or Vi Petty. As Jerry Allison subsequently noted, 'Buddy thought the organ was more suitable for church.' Norman Petty claims the responsibility for suggesting the idea, adding that there was no way he could have forced it on Holly if the latter did not want to use it—'he was as stubborn a person as I ever met in my life—I couldn't convince him to do anything he didn't want to do'.

It was Petty, of course, who had previously added the celeste to *Everyday* and his vision can only be applauded in both instances. A keyboard was also used on the two songs recorded at this session that would be released under the name of the Crickets, although in the case of *Fool's Paradise* only as a subsidiary instrument. This song must qualify, together with *Take Your Time,* as one of the lesser known Holly tracks. *Fool's Paradise* was first released as the B-side of the fourth Crickets single, *Think It Over,* cut at the same time, but on this latter recording the piano part is definitely the work of Vi Petty. As her husband later said, 'Vi was really playing hard with her left hand, because she was annoyed with me. You see, she'd had formal musical training, so I expected her to be able to play what I suggested first time, and if she didn't grasp it immediately, I'd get cross with her.' The result was a magnificent track which was a hit for the Crickets on both sides of the Atlantic, following *Rave On,* which had been released a few weeks earlier, up the chart during the early summer of 1958. In America, even *Fool's Paradise* made the chart for a short time, one of the few occasions when both sides of a record by Buddy or the Crickets was recognised as a hit, although every track released as a single, with the possible exception of *Mailman Bring Me No More Blues,* had been eminently worthy of hit status.

The final track cut at this session did not feature piano. Credited to Holly, Allison, Mauldin and Petty, and apparently the only song on which all

THEY'RE COMING

PAUL ANKA and . . .

IT is no good trying to write off Paul Anka as a fluke. Anyone who attempts it is precisely two hit songs too late.

Whatever you think about his first composition, "Diana," the fact has to be faced that it must have contained an element missing from cleverer numbers. Probably it was in touch with both the times *and* the teenage market.

Getting into the best sellers a second time with "You Are My Destiny" somehow proves something for Master Anka. And when a smart impresario like Harold Fielding books him for a second concert tour of Britain—he has 23 concerts opening on March 1 at Aberdeen—then we grey-beards have to do a little reassessing.

I have canvassed opinions among those who met Anka last time to counter-balance my memories of his "Sunday Night At The London Palladium" appearance. "What's he like?" I asked a colleague of mine.

Little gentleman

"Well, I'm bound to say this:

"He's a real little gentleman. When I walked into his dressing room he leaped to his feet and said: 'Good evening, Sir.' After meeting one of the American teenage 'stars,' I had been expecting something in the nature of a precocious brat.

"What I found was a homesick boy who told me how much he was missing his kid sister and brother."

There was no act about it. Anka had been away from home for two months. His father (Paul calls him Andy) hadn't been able to accompany him to England. So the 16-year-old faced the terrors of early fame alone.

Of course, he had his professional helpers. But who among them spoke his language?

It won't be so terrible this time. Andy should be on hand and Anka, having proved his mettle once, should have gained confidence. Certainly he can expect to meet plenty of friends.—**Tony Brown.**

. . . THE CRICKETS

BUDDY HOLLY and the Crickets have been given a VIP greeting on their first trip to Britain.

They have been booked straight into ATV's "Sunday Night At The London Palladium" following their opening date at the Trocadero, Elephant and Castle, tomorrow (Saturday).

Decca's Coral label has also not been slow to pay tribute to the group that has paid off so handsomely disc-wise. Holly's new solo recording of "Listen To Me" and "I'm Gonna Love You Too" is out today (Coral Q72288).

Big hopes

And the collective Crickets offer "Tell Me How" and "Maybe Baby"—introduced on "Six-Five Special" last Saturday—the same day (Coral Q72307). Decca's Tony Hall has big hopes for the "Baby" side.

Arriving with the Crickets at London Airport this afternoon — at 2.45 p.m.—is manager Norman Petty.

Holly and the boys understandably think a lot of Petty. And they pay direct tribute to Elvis Presley for "paving the way" for their eventual success. "A great vocal artist in his field," they chirp in unison.—**Laurie Henshaw.**

four collaborated, it was *Well . . . All Right*. The song's title was apparently the frequently-used catch phrase of Little Richard, although the Holly version certainly did not reflect the exuberance of Richard Penniman, being a gently reflective love song.

By the time that *Rave On/Take Your Time* and *Think It Over/Fool's Paradise* were released and had made their mark in the charts, a peculiar syndrome had emerged. In every case, with the exception of *Peggy Sue/Everyday*, British chart placings had always been on average higher than those achieved in America. The reason for this comparative rejection by Holly's own country can only be guessed at, but perhaps the fact that the Crickets were one of the first rock'n'roll acts from America to tour Britain may be significant. Certainly, those who saw that tour remember it with great affection, and it is also possible that the many budding British guitarists who attended to watch the style of Holly's playing were heartened by the fact that Holly, although able to produce magnificent solos and fills, was untutored enough in his technique to use a capo on his guitar. The capo, a device normally used by folk club performers, allows the guitarist to change key without altering the shape of the chords formed by his left hand.

On the group's return from the Alan Freed package tour in mid-May 1958, Buddy Holly took part in one of the most unusual recordings with which he was ever associated. He acted as a session player for a record made by Jerry Allison under the name of 'Ivan', Allison's middle name. The two tracks which form the record are *Real Wild Child* and *Oh You Beautiful Doll*. The latter was intended as a humorous version of the old standard, although twenty years on, it doesn't seem particularly funny. On the other hand, *Real Wild Child* is highly enjoyable, bearing many of the trademarks of a Crickets' backing track. Holly played guitar and Mauldin bass, but as Allison was concentrating on his vocals, the drums were played by Bo Clarke, another musician who often played at Petty's studio. The A-side was a song which the Crickets had heard in Australia sung by Johnny O'Keefe, the young Australian star whom the group had befriended. It was released in America as the Crickets' record company was willing to put out anything connected with the group, and briefly entered the lower half of the chart, although it failed to equal that success in Britain. Holly's participation in the recording was not common knowledge at the time of release, which has meant that it is now regarded as something of a collector's item.

'We used Hammond organ on 'Take Your Time', sort of against Buddy's better judgement, because he felt that organ was to be reserved for church.'

June 1958 was a month which, in retrospect, became one of the most important in Buddy Holly's short life. He and Petty went to New York on business, and while they were there, Holly went into a recording studio to cut two tracks. For the first time since coming to fame, the Crickets were not providing instrumental backing and, perhaps more important, Petty was not the producer of the session.

The songs were both written by Bobby Darin, who had not yet made a hit record and was on the point of being dropped by his record company, Atco (a subsidiary of Atlantic Records) after singles like *Million Dollar Baby, Don't Call My Name* and *Just In Case You Change Your Mind* had failed to penetrate the magic chart. At the time of Holly's visit to New York, Darin was negotiating with Brunswick for a new contract on the strength of two songs, and in order not to excite Atlantic into litigation, they were to be released on Brunswick under the name of his backing group, the Rinky Dinks. But at the last moment, Atco's final attempt at scoring a hit with Darin, *Splish Splash*, took off

Right: Buddy photographed during the sessions at Bell Sound Studios in January 1958, when 'Rave On' was produced. Top left: In the British pop papers, the Crickets took second place to Paul Anka.

Left: Buddy on the British TV programme 'Sunday Night at the London Palladium'.
Above: Bob Thiele of Coral presenting Buddy and Norman Petty with a gold disc for 'Peggy Sue'.

in a big way and reached number three in America. Atco logically decided that it would be folly to drop Darin, and exercised their right to his already recorded version of *Early In The Morning* which Darin had made while under contract to them. It was still released under the name of the Rinky Dinks to avoid confusion with *Splish Splash,* whereupon both records were sizeable hits. This left Brunswick with a pair of songs which they considered potential hits, but with no artist to record them. The arrival in New York of Holly and Petty was particularly timely, and when Petty heard of the company's predicament, he suggested that Holly should record them if he was agreeable.

Holly was quite willing, possibly because he was interested in making a record on his own for a change, although there is no reason to suspect that at this stage the relationship between Holly and Petty was turning sour. The producer of the session was Dick Jacobs, a Decca employee who had also produced the original Darin version. As backing musicians, Jacobs hired a number of experienced New York session players. The recordings were made at a studio known as the Pythian Temple, which allowed the musicians and backing singers, a gospel group known as the Helen Way Singers, to perform on a stage with Holly in front of them singing, although not playing guitar. The names of most of the musicians have been forgotten, although it is probable that the drummer was Panama Francis, while the saxophone, which had not been used before on Holly recordings, was played by Sam 'The Man' Taylor. The absence of the Crickets did not worry Holly, as the song obviously required a more gospel styled backing than perhaps Allison and Mauldin would have been capable of providing, and there is no doubt that the record is one of the most energetic Holly ever recorded. Norman Petty, who was present at the session as an observer, remembered recently, '*Early In The Morning* was one of the most exciting and fun records Buddy ever made', although he perhaps did not realise that it was contributing to his own separation from his protégé. Buddy too, appears to have particularly liked this recording. According to Jerry Allison, 'He really thought it was an excellent record. He liked having the black chorus singing on it.' As for *Now We're One,* it's doubtful Holly would have bothered with such a basically insubstantial item had it not been presented in a package with *Early In The Morning.*

On another trip to New York in June 1958, a crucial event occurred. While the group were visiting their music publishers, Southern Music, Buddy Holly met and fell in love with a Puerto Rican girl, Maria Elena Santiago. Maria was working at Southern Music (where her aunt was an executive in charge of the Latin American division). The Crickets came in to see Murray Deutsch, and had to wait in the outer office where Maria worked as Deutsch's receptionist. Buddy was immediately

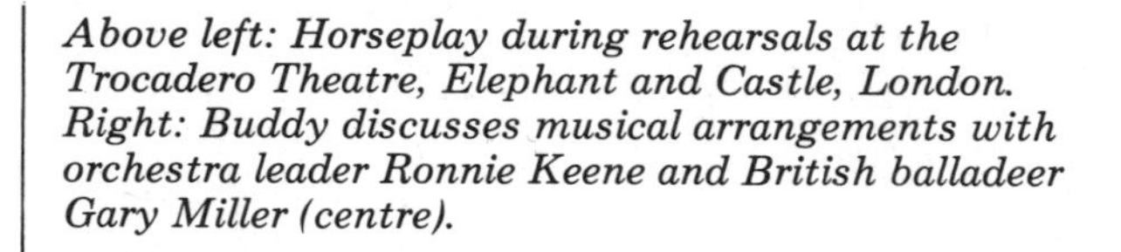

Above left: Horseplay during rehearsals at the Trocadero Theatre, Elephant and Castle, London. Right: Buddy discusses musical arrangements with orchestra leader Ronnie Keene and British balladeer Gary Miller (centre).

attracted to her, and on coming out of his meeting with Deutsch, invited her to lunch. Maria describes her reaction: 'Well, when you're a receptionist, you're supposed to greet people and be pleasant to them, and not take everything they say too seriously. So I told him I wouldn't be free for a couple of hours. "OK", he said, "we'll be waiting for you." And I thought that was just part of their joking around.'

It wasn't. Holly managed to get Maria down to the restaurant where they were having lunch. At one point during the meal, Maria Elena remembers Buddy Holly saying: 'You see this girl. I'm going to marry her. And I'm going to get her to agree in the next few days, before we leave New York.' Holly asked Maria out for that evening. Her aunt, however, who had looked after Maria ever since her mother had died when she was eight, was very protective of her charge and familiar enough with the music business to find the prospect of her niece befriending a musician somewhat undesirable. But Maria, intrigued by Holly's enthusiasm, prevailed upon her aunt to allow the date to go ahead, during the course of which Buddy proposed marriage. 'I guess it sounds crazy', explains Maria, 'that he should propose and I should accept, the very day we met. But that's what really happened—we just each felt that way, that quickly.' The next day, although she knew she wanted to marry him, Maria Elena asked Holly whether he wouldn't rather think it over for a while. But Holly was adamant—he was sure he wanted to marry her.

The proposed union was not likely to be one which in the eyes of either family would seem to have been made in heaven. Maria Elena was a Puerto Rican, although her roots were much closer to the high society of her race than the familiar film portrayal of Puerto Ricans as inhabitants of overcrowded tenements situated in slum areas. Being of Spanish extraction she was also a Catholic, which conflicted with the Holley family's beliefs. The Fundamentalist Baptist faith strongly opposed marriages where different races or different faiths were concerned, and no doubt Maria Elena's family felt the same. However, she readily agreed to become Mrs Buddy Holly, and a wedding date was set for August 15th, 1958, the end of the Crickets' current tour and just two months after the couple had met. Buddy and Maria Elena were married in Lubbock by Buddy's pastor, Ben Johnson, before his family and a few friends, including Jerry and Peggy Sue Allison, who had themselves got married a few weeks earlier. In fact, the Allisons accompanied the Hollys on a joint honeymoon in Acapulco.

‘You see this girl? I'm going to marry her: I'm going to get her to agree before we leave New York.’

Being married did not slow down Buddy Holly's phenomenal work rate, nor his ambition to be successful in as many facets of the music business as possible. Having written a number of hit songs for himself and the Crickets, Buddy decided to try writing a hit for someone else, in this case his friends the Everly Brothers, with whom the Crickets had shared bills on several occasions. While he had been in Lubbock during that summer, Buddy had contacted his old friend Bob Montgomery and suggested that they collaborate. He probably thought that Montgomery's known bias towards country music might invest the project with greater credibility in the eyes of the Everly Brothers, whose inclination was more towards country than rock'n'roll.

The reunited team initially composed two songs, *Love's Made A Fool Of You* and *Wishing*. In order

Right: Buddy and Maria on their wedding day, August 15th 1958. Inset: With Jerry and Peggy Sue Allison on joint honeymoon in Acapulco.

to present them properly to the Everlys, Holly decided to record demos of the songs himself in Norman Petty's studio, with full instrumental backing. However, as it was not intended that the recordings should ever be unleashed on the public, the Crickets were not asked to play on the tracks, and instrumental backing was provided by three session musicians who would work with anyone who needed them at Petty's studio. Bo Clarke, who had played drums instead of Jerry Allison on the *Real Wild Child* session, again helped out, while the bass player was George Atwood, a man in his thirties with a background in jazz rather than popular music. The guitarist hired to allow Holly to concentrate on his singing was Tommy Allsup, an Oklahoman, who had first come to Clovis to play on a session for another artist, but had impressed Petty enough to be invited to stay.

The session went very well, but as luck would have it, Holly had not considered the attitude of the Everlys' manager, Wesley Rose of Acuff-Rose Music. Rose was the kind of manager who would generally only allow his artists to record a song in which his publishing company had an interest, especially if it were designed for release as a single. Such behaviour was by no means unique. As the normal arrangement was that publishing royalties were split equally between the songwriter and his

Left and below: Buddy and the Crickets on BBC TV's 'Off the Record', a sequence specially recorded for national transmission after the group left Britain for America.

Above: At the press reception at the start of the Crickets' British tour, the Crickets posed with two of England's foremost Test cricketers, Godfrey Evans and Denis Compton.

publishing company, most managers felt there was no reason to give large sums of money to an outsider, when the money could be retained within the organisation. When Holly's two demos were received by Wesley Rose, he may have sensed that he might be presenting an advantage to a competitor (Norman Petty), were he to allow his charges to record a Holly song, even though *Love's Made A Fool Of You* was very suitable material for the Everlys. As a result, Holly's first attempt at customising a song for another artist was a disappointment.

Around the same time, the Crickets went into Norman Petty's studio to cut some new tracks which *were* intended for release. Two were recorded which would be Crickets songs, Holly and Petty's excellent *It's So Easy,* which was strangely unsuccessful when released as a single, and *Lonesome Tears.* Tommy Allsup also participated in this session, and played on the recording of the other song taped at this time, *Heartbeat.* This was a collaboration between Bob Montgomery and Norman Petty designed as a Buddy Holly solo release, with George Atwood playing bass in the temporary absence of Joe Mauldin. *Heartbeat* was another comparative disaster when it was eventually released as the follow up Buddy Holly single to *Early In The Morning/Now We're One*, which had been fairly successful, reaching the top thirty in America, and the top twenty in Britain. The problem with *Heartbeat* was that it was virtually impossible to dance to, having a Latin-American rhythm similar to the Beguine.

During September 1958, there was more action in the Clovis studio involving Buddy Holly with two

NME critics review package show

HOLLY-CRICKETS give us loudest rock show yet!

By KEITH GOODWIN

Gary Miller's night drive in Cyprus was too thrilling!

Centre: Buddy's first solo album sleeve, released March 1958. Above: An enthusiastic review in England's 'New Musical Express'.

Buddy and the Crickets toured with Alan Freed's nationwide 'Big Show of 1958', dubbed 'The Big Beat' by journalists. L. to r.: Alan Freed, Larry Williams, and Buddy.

new musicians, Waylon Jennings and King Curtis. Jennings was a disc jockey in Lubbock when he was introduced to Buddy by 'Hipockets' Duncan, who had first encouraged Holly and Bob Montgomery back in the days of the Buddy and Bob Group. 'Hipockets' had seen in Jennings another potential star and he asked Holly if there was anything he might be able to do to assist. Holly was reportedly impressed and agreed to arrange for Jennings to make a record.

Holly had had continuous exposure to black music via the many black acts with whom he had toured over the previous months. He had been especially impressed by the Coasters, and in particular with their brilliant saxophone player, King Curtis. In order that Curtis should be available to help Holly experiment with the saxophone on this recording, Holly arranged to pay Curtis' expenses for a short trip to Clovis. It was Curtis who was responsible for several of the classic rock'n'roll moments involving the saxophone, such as his electrifying break on the Coasters' *Yakety Yak,* which had been number one in the American chart a few weeks before. The first Buddy Holly record which had included a saxophone was *Early In The Morning*, and Holly was interested in its many possibilities. On this occasion, two songs were recorded, *Reminiscing*, which Curtis himself had written, and its eventual B-side, *Come Back Baby*, which was the joint work of Norman Petty and Fred Neil. Neil was born in Florida but left there in the late fifties, moving to the Nashville area, where he had probably met Petty. He found his greatest fame during the sixties after he had moved to New York, and was recognized as a gifted writer on the strength of songs like *Everybody's Talkin'*, which was an enormous hit for Harry Nilsson, who sang it for the soundtrack of the film *Midnight Cowboy*. However, *Come Back Baby* is not one of Neil's most inspired songs, and it is only lifted above average by characteristically fluid work from Curtis and a thoughtful vocal from Holly. *Reminiscing*, on the other hand, is a far better song, and the recording made by Holly, Curtis, Mauldin and Allison remains one of the best ever Holly tracks.

As Curtis was at Clovis, Buddy also decided to use him on the songs he was going to produce for Waylon Jennings. This was probably Holly's first formal experience as producer, although it seems that he had frequently contributed production ideas when working with Petty, and was far from a novice on the subject. For the two songs that were recorded—the Cajun classic *Jole Blon* and a song written by two local writers called *When Sin Stops*—Holly played guitar, while George Atwood and Bo Clarke formed the rhythm section. When it was released on Brunswick the record was a flop, although the fact that Holly was involved in them has subsequently given the tracks a somewhat greater importance than perhaps they deserve. Waylon Jennings has for many years refused to talk about his connection with Buddy Holly, feeling that too great an emphasis has been put on

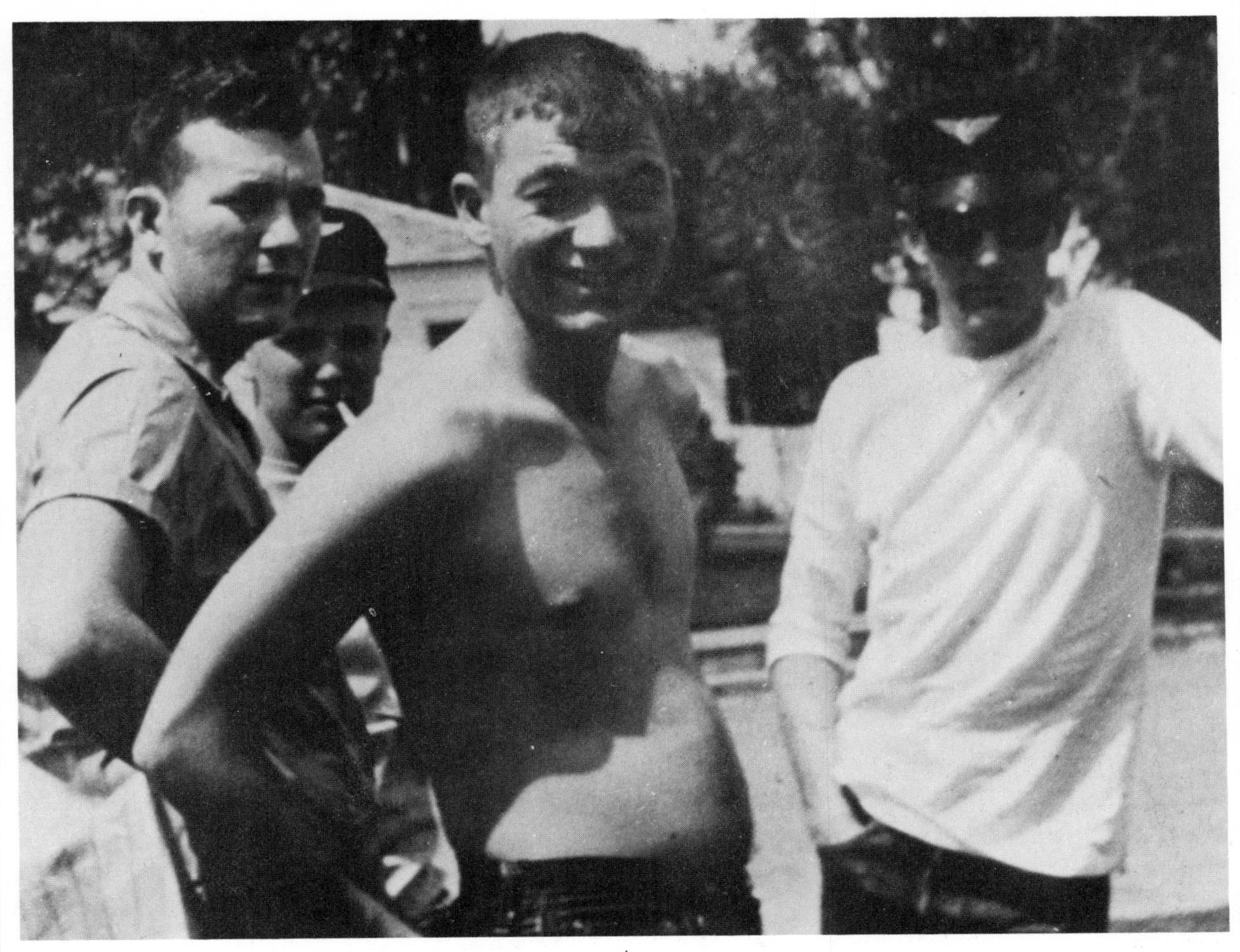

what had been, for him, a relatively brief interlude in his career. He has subsequently become a superstar of country music, and one of the forerunners of the 'Outlaw' movement, a group of musicians who refuse to abide by the traditional rules of Nashville and have established their own country music headquarters in Austin, Texas.

The relative failure of many of Holly's and the Crickets' singles in America during the middle months of 1958 may have been the reason for Buddy's decision, on a visit to New York in October 1958, to try recording with an orchestra. The prevailing tide in music had moved away from all-out rock'n'roll towards a more balladic approach, as indicated by the top records of the year—*All I Have To Do Is Dream* by the Everly Brothers, *Don't* by Elvis Presley and *It's Only Make Believe* by Conway Twitty, and first hits for a new breed of less frantic rockers than the class of '56, artists like Connie Francis and Sam Cooke. If one of Holly's records was not as successful as he thought it should have been, he would analyse the reasons for its failure, and try to correct what was wrong for his next studio session. *It's So Easy* had shown no sign of cracking open the chart, and its resemblance, at least superficially, to *That'll Be The Day* may have occurred to Holly as a reason for its lack of success. With Presley moving away from full-time rock'n'roll, perhaps Holly felt that he too should move on to orchestral-backed numbers.

Time off in Lubbock: Buddy (in dark glasses) with Jerry Allison (centre), Norman Petty and Joe Mauldin in the background.

Holly's return to Pythian Temple in October was to be his last recording session in a properly equipped studio, although of course he did not know it at the time. Once again, Dick Jacobs produced the session, but this time, instead of the predominantly black session players and gospel singers, Holly's backing was provided by an orchestra, nominally the Dick Jacobs Orchestra, but most likely a team of experienced session men who would turn themselves into the orchestra of whoever was paying them. Again, Holly did not play guitar, preferring to concentrate on his singing. The four tracks cut on this occasion were *True Love Ways, Moondreams, Raining In My Heart,* and *It Doesn't Matter Anymore;* two from within the Holly camp, and two which originated from elsewhere. The latter pair would become within a few months two of the most well-known songs Holly recorded. *It Doesn't Matter Anymore* was a last minute inclusion in the session, as its writer, Paul Anka, had only completed the song a matter of hours before Holly was due to record it. Anka had become friendly with the Crickets during the time when both acts were touring for long periods together, and although he was only eighteen years old at the time, he was already a veteran of the

music business. Dick Jacobs describes the famous last minute rush to include this song: 'At about six-thirty Buddy came dashing into my office and said, "Dick, I hate to do this to you, but Paul Anka has just played me a fantastic song, and we have to do it on the session tonight" . . . Buddy and I sat in my office right there and then and I wrote out an arrangement . . . I had no time to write anything but a unison pizzicato thing.' This 'pizzicato thing' is generally regarded as the very first rock'n'roll record to feature string accompaniment, together with its equally famous B-side, *Raining In My Heart,* which was also a song from outside Holly's immediate circle. *Raining In My Heart* was written by the husband and wife team who were probably the Everlys' manager Wesley Rose's hottest property in song-writing terms, Boudleux and Felice Bryant.

The other two songs recorded at the session also featured the orchestra, and were *True Love Ways*, a Holly/Petty collaboration, and *Moondreams,* a Norman Petty song. The predominant impression left by all four tracks is of Buddy Holly aiming in a rather different direction, propelled by the very sweet backing of the orchestra. The contrast between these tracks and the far noisier backings laid down by the Crickets is enormous—the keyword has altered from 'excitement' to 'sophistication', and the appeal from a teenage audience to an older and more romantic (but also larger and more opulent) group of record buyers. Perhaps Norman Petty had subliminally suggested to Buddy Holly that the time was right to branch out, being far more familiar with 'easy listening' music than with rock'n'roll, and believing that Holly would continue to rely on him to some extent for advice. Whether or not Buddy Holly would have continued in this new direction had he lived can only be a matter for conjecture, although many Holly experts tend to feel that it would have been a shortlived experiment, and that Holly would have returned to the rock'n' roll with which he was more at home, and with

'He used to sing 'True Love Ways' to me all the time before he died. It was our secret song.'

which, after all, he had initially become famous.

Buddy's marriage to Maria Elena had meanwhile made relations between Norman Petty and Holly extremely strained. Petty had been against any of the Crickets getting married, as he felt he would lose control over their affairs. Maria Elena, having worked in the centre of the music industry in New York, was considerably more familiar with its workings than either Holly or Petty, and when Buddy decided to break with Petty, she gave him

In the summer of 1958 the Crickets blew some tour money to realize a long-standing ambition: they each bought a brand new motor-cycle.

full encouragement. Petty is quoted as asking Buddy what he had done wrong, to which Maria Elena gave the answer: 'It's not what you've done, it's what you haven't done'. Maria's acquaintance with the music publishing business may have led her to feel, as others have since, that Petty's handling of the Crickets' finances and publishing was unorthodox, in that he had continued to add his own name to credits where he may not have deserved inclusion. That aside, there are other items with which Maria Elena felt unhappy. For example, it seems that Norman Petty refused to spend any income on advertising new records by Buddy or the Crickets in the American trade magazines, which during the fifties was almost obligatory, although, in Petty's defence, probably a waste of money. The result was that Holly's record company paid for the advertisements, deducting the cost from royalties, whereas if Petty had paid, the royalties received would have been greater, while the cost of the advertising could have been offset against tax. Another item to which Maria took particular exception was again in the realm of publicity—it appears that until she arrived on the scene, all publicity photographs of Holly or the Crickets had been taken by Petty himself rather than by a professional photographer. When Buddy split from Petty, Maria quickly got him into a studio in New York where many of the famous portraits of him were taken.

‘I liked show business. I wanted to be part of what Buddy did. I wanted to be active . . . like answering the fan mail and organising fan clubs.’

Prior to Maria becoming Mrs Holly, there had been few, if any, signs that Holly was in any way discontented with Norman Petty as a mentor, but Maria's encouragement that he should disentangle himself from his manager might have carried far less weight had Holly not recorded successfully, on two separate occasions, with Dick Jacobs. Since his unsympathetic reception in Nashville, Holly had come to rely on Petty as his record producer and if Petty had had an inkling of what might transpire, it seems highly unlikely that he would have allowed Holly to work with anyone else. Once Maria came along, Buddy appears to have regretted ever having associated with Petty, in spite of Petty's direct influence on his success. Hipockets Duncan reported him as saying angrily, 'Hipockets, I wish a thousand times I had talked with you before I got involved with that man.' Buddy's father, who has always been close to Maria, believed Maria was just what Buddy needed. Buddy had a tendency to rely on people and until she came along it was not always to his advantage. Mr Holley believed that Maria was the best thing that ever happened to Buddy. 'When he was younger', he told her, 'he was tied to his mother, then he was tied to Norman Petty; but now he's come into his own—he's finally a man.'

Left: Buddy Holly with his treasured Fender Stratocaster. His constant use of the instrument helped to boost the popularity of this model. Above: Maria Elena Holly used her inside knowledge of the business to help Buddy embark on his solo career.

Another important factor in Buddy's move away from Petty was that Maria Elena had been brought up in big city surroundings, and was less able to adapt to the quieter life of Lubbock. She urged Buddy to let them move to New York, and as Holly was keen to progress musically, he welcomed the chance to base himself near the centre of the industry. A ready-made replacement for Petty was available in New York to deal with Holly's affairs. This was Irving Fell, who was President of a major booking agency and also managed Paul Anka.

There was still the question of the Crickets to be resolved. The group had grown back to four members again with the addition of Tommy Allsup. Apart from Holly's appreciation of his guitar playing talent, Allsup was a little older than the rest, which meant that he was able to buy drinks for the band in states where nobody under the age of twenty-one was allowed by law to purchase liquor. As the only member over twenty-one, Holly probably felt that it would be a weight removed if someone else could assist in satisfying the thirsts of Jerry Allison and Joe Mauldin, who were both still teenagers in 1958 but already quite heavy drinkers.

In October, following an Alan Freed TV show and then a GAC package tour with Eddie Cochran, Bobby Darin, Frankie Avalon, Clyde McPhatter and the Coasters, Holly made the decision to move to New York. At the same time he asked the other Crickets whether they wanted to remain with him and break with Petty, in which case it would be better if they too lived on the East Coast. Allsup, who had travelled around more than the others, was quite amenable to the idea, and in fact stayed in New York for some time after Holly's death, but the others, who were still living at home, were less certain. Holly's and Allison's marriages already meant that the group was less close, rarely coming together except to play. Eventually Allison and Mauldin decided to make the move with Buddy, but returned to Lubbock after the October tour to collect their possessions. While they were there, they went to Clovis to see Norman Petty, who talked them out of going, suggesting that the Crickets would still be a viable proposition even without Buddy Holly. Doubtless feeling insecure at the thought of moving permanently away from their families, Allison and Mauldin agreed to stay with Petty, an additional persuasive factor being that the Crickets had scored rather more hit records as a group than Holly had solo.

Disappointed but not discouraged, Buddy Holly returned to New York without most of his band. He and Maria had taken an apartment close to Greenwich Village. But he did little formal work for the rest of 1958. Part of his time was spent designing furniture for the apartment, and even taking drama coaching, and because the Hollys had not been able to install a piano at that time, Buddy would go to the apartment owned by Maria's aunt from Southern Music, and use her instrument to compose new songs. Among those which were originated in this

‘Norman wanted Buddy to come back . . . that's why he wanted the Crickets to stay. I don't think he thought he had any great talent in me and Joe B.’

Buddy, Jerry and Joe B. at the height of the Crickets' fame. In October 1958 the group split.

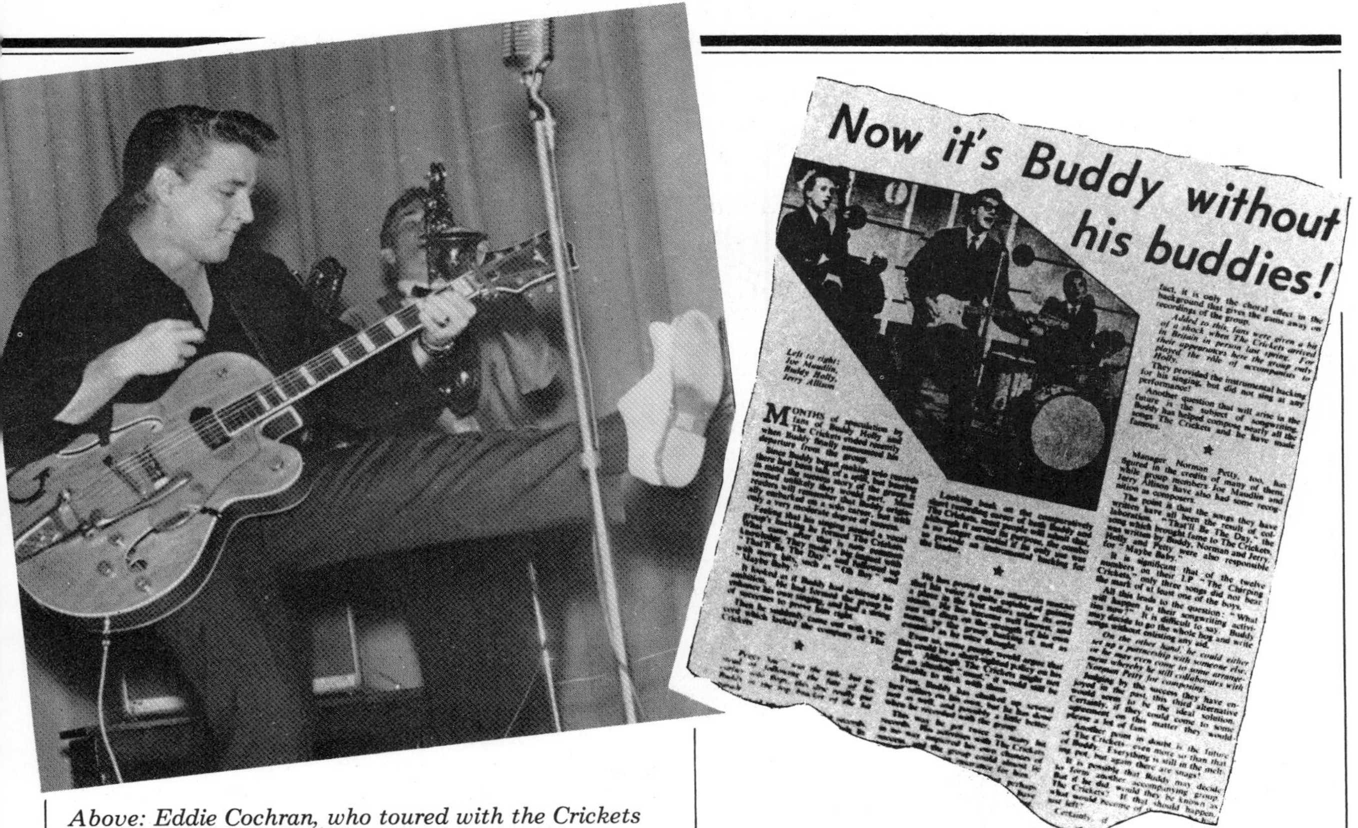

Now it's Buddy without his buddies!

Left to right: Joe Mauldin, Buddy Holly, Jerry Allison

Above: Eddie Cochran, who toured with the Crickets on their last joint GAC rock'n'roll circus. Above right: The music press tells the Holly solo story. Below: Maria Elena engaged a New York showbiz photographer to take new publicity shots of Buddy in the winter of 1958.

manner were *Peggy Sue Got Married* and *Stay Close to Me*, which appears to be the only song which Buddy Holly wrote but never recorded. Instead, it was recorded by Lou Giordano.

Holly's work as an independent producer for Brunswick continued with this single by Giordano, but it was just as unsuccessful as his previous attempt with Waylon Jennings. Unlike Jennings, Giordano faded into obscurity almost immediately afterwards.

Most of the time during those last two months of 1958 was spent in being a newly married husband. Up to that point, there had been little time for Buddy and Maria to be together without being part of a crowd or on tour, where Maria posed as Buddy's secretary, in order, it is said, that his unpublicised marriage should not antagonise his fans. Holly was also making plans for future projects. The single of *Heartbeat/Well . . . All Right* was not proving to be a success, taking nearly two months to enter the charts in America, and a similar period in Britain, while the final Crickets single, *It's So Easy,* had failed to make the chart in any way.

Most of Holly's activity was not in public, although at Christmas 1958, when Buddy and Maria went back to Lubbock, he called in to see his friends at the local radio station. While he was there he decided to improvise a new song on the spot, a somewhat insubstantial number called *You're The One.* The only instrumentation was Buddy's guitar with which he accompanied himself. Handclapping was provided by Waylon Jennings, who was still

working on the radio station, and Slim Corbin, who was part owner of the station. The resulting recording was released much later with additional backing, but is far from being a milestone in Buddy Holly's musical career, and was not intended as such—the real purpose of the visit to Lubbock was to spend Christmas 1958 among Buddy's family and friends.

The Day The Music Died-1959

CHAPTER FOUR

When Mr and Mrs Charles Hardin Holley returned to New York at the start of the new year, they were faced with a problem which could have adversely affected all their plans—a shortage of ready cash. The one miscalculation that had been made when it was decided to split with Norman Petty was that he, as manager of Buddy and the Crickets, had been the recipient of all the group's record royalties. Neither Buddy nor any of the other Crickets had received money regularly from Petty. Occasionally he would hand over amount for special occasions, such as the Crickets' purchase of motor-cycles in the summer of '58. But generally, Petty seems to have treated the money which the group earned with a proprietorial interest—nothing could be withdrawn from the group's bank account without his approval. The situation became even more intractable when Holly removed managerial responsiblities from Petty, as the latter refused to allow Holly any money due to him until the complex accounts of the terminated relationship were professionally worked out. Petty had every legal right to take this course of action, as many other managers have done in similar circumstances. By the same token, it is quite likely that the thought occurred to Petty that were Holly sufficiently squeezed financially, he might be forced to change his mind and come back to Petty's management.

Buddy Holly, however, was not a person to be held to ransom—having gained his independence he was not about to lose it again in this manner. Holly's refusal to do anything which he did not want, as Norman Petty had experienced earlier when attempting to change the sound of Holly's recordings, amounted to extreme stubbornness. That stubborn streak made Buddy Holly look at alternative methods of financial survival—anything rather than crawl back to Petty's fold. The most obvious method was to go back on the road—after all, a proven hitmaker was much in demand, and with more than half a dozen under his belt, Holly could certainly claim to be among that élite. In other circumstances, the strain of the one-night stand circuit might have been a thing of the past for Holly, but his enormous desire to succeed, further fuelled by his wife's encouragement, drove him to dismiss any thoughts of relaxation from his mind. Apart from composing some new material for forthcoming records, Buddy also had his production agreement with Brunswick and was about to start his own music publishing company with his wife's help and bearing her name—Maria Music.

‘I can't say that the words or the music came first. He did them together.’

During January 1959, Buddy worked hard at songwriting, knocking half a dozen new songs into shape, and recording rough demos of them. *That's What They Say, What To Do, Peggy Sue Got Married, That Makes It Tough, Learning The Game* and *Crying, Waiting, Hoping* were to be the last songs that Holly would write, but the high standards he had set himself over previous months were maintained. One or two of the songs even indicated an improvement on previous output. One of the projects upon which Holly was working was to collaborate with black R&B singer Ray Charles, whom Holly wanted to use as his producer. At least one of the new songs, *That Makes It Tough*, was written for the Charles project, and the same may be

Left: The Crickets after the split with Holly. From top: Jerry Allison, Sonny Curtis, Joe B. Mauldin. Below: Holly on the Winter Dance Party tour with, l. to r.: Jim Lounsbury of WBKB-TV, the Big Bopper, Debbie Stevens and Frankie Sardo.

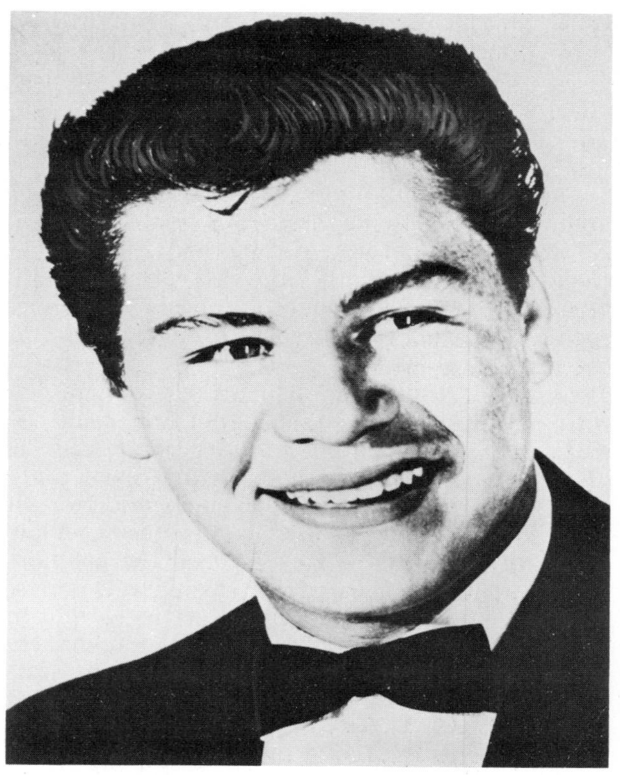

Above: The Big Bopper. Right: Ritchie Valens. Both died with Buddy Holly.

true of two of the others, *Learning The Game* and *Crying, Waiting, Hoping,* which are written around themes of universal lost love much in the manner of the burgeoning wistfulness which characterised rhythm and blues at the time.

However, on the one occasion when Buddy and Maria did try to seek out the blind musician, they spent hours getting through the various security devices which surrounded Charles' Los Angeles home, only to find when they reached the front door that Charles was away on tour.

Two of the others, *That's What They Say* and *What To Do,* are rather less well-known, though by no means inferior. The final song of the six, *Peggy Sue Got Married,* indicates that Buddy was not averse to copying the tricks used by others in his attempts to achieve hit records by using the 'answer song' convention. *Peggy Sue Got Married* adds a slightly new slant to the 'answer' idea, with lines like 'Do you recall the girl that's been in nearly every song?' Holly may have written the song as part of his effort to get back on good terms with Jerry Allison, although it seems that the idea for the song came from Buddy's father. When it was released as a single after Holly's death, it became one of his biggest posthumous hits, bigger in fact than any of the other originals taped during the same period.

The six new songs, assigned to Maria Music, were not the sum total of Holly's recordings during the last weeks of his life. Perhaps again with the Ray Charles project in mind, Buddy recorded six other tracks which had been made famous by others, including two versions of Little Richard's *Slippin' and Slidin',* one fast and one slow. The last version utilises the familiar guitar riff from *Bird Dog* by the Everly Brothers, and more or less follows the Little Richard original. The slow version is quite unlike any other recording of the song, a reinterpretation which owes much to soul music. Holly was concentrating on black music at this time; he also returned to Bo Diddley for inspiration—having recorded Diddley's eponymous theme back in 1956, he now recorded *Dearest* (this version sometimes being known as 'Umm Oh Yeah', approximating to some soulful mumbling by Holly within the song.) Still more black music came via one of Holly's favourite groups, the Coasters. Prior to adopting that name in 1957, the Coasters had been known as the Robins, and in that guise had recorded *Smokey Joe's Cafe,* another song which Holly chose to cover at this time, although neither that song nor *Dearest* were particularly successful.

By far the most interesting of these cover versions is Holly's treatment of the music hall song *Wait Till The Sun Shines Nellie.* This incongruous song was recorded for his mother—it was one of her favourites, although her son's strikingly different arrangement may not quite have been what she had in mind. Even so, the song is amazingly successful in rock'n'roll terms, and it may also have inspired him to compose *That's What They Say.* The final song of the half dozen was *Love Is Strange,* the work of black artists Mickey and Sylvia, although it later became a hit for more than one white artist. When the recording of the song was finally released, Holly's version was introduced by a guitar passage very similar to the one which begins *Words Of Love,* which may have been added after his death by Norman Petty.

It is difficult to assess exactly when these final recordings were made, as all were made on a domestic tape recorder. But Tommy Allsup maintains that he helped to record *Peggy Sue Got Married* and *That Makes It Tough*, adding guitar licks behind Buddy's voice, on the night before they were to leave New York to embark on the fateful tour during which Buddy died.

Buddy Holly had a choice of several different tours to select from, had he been slightly less impatient to stand on his own feet financially. The 'Winter Dance Party', as it was called, was one of the least desirable packages imaginable, but he agreed to go because it meant ready money. The venues to be played were in the Mid-West where the winter is always unpleasant, and travelling is an uncomfortable and hazardous occupation. On the opening dates of the tour, appalling weather conditions had so badly affected the roads, that the performers had been marooned in snowstorms after the tour bus had broken down, and the drummer whom Holly had selected to stand in for Jerry Allison, session player Charlie Bunch, had to be taken into hospital with frostbite.

‘Buddy went on the tour as a favour to GAC: they needed a bigger attraction on the bill. Of course the money was a reason for going, as well.’

The bill for 'The Winter Dance Party' was somewhat less sensational than some of the earlier tours which Holly had played with the Crickets. Two of the artists, Ritchie Valens and the Big Bopper, had recently achieved their first hits, and the other two acts, Frankie Sardo and Dion and the Belmonts, had yet to do that. Ritchie Valens was a seventeen-year-old kid from Los Angeles with a distinct resemblance to film star Glenn Ford. He had written a song about his girl friend, *Donna,* and achieved a number two hit with it, his second record. Valens had just released the follow up, a Mexican item titled *La Bamba,* which would be his second hit, although Ritchie would never know about it. J. P. Richardson was a Texan disc jockey and songwriter. In his *nom de radio,* the Big Bopper, Richardson had recorded a novelty song a few months before called *Chantilly Lace,* which had climbed into the top ten, reaching a million sales, and he was also promoting a new single, *Big Bopper's Wedding.* As a songwriter, Richardson's greatest success was to be posthumous, in the shape of *Running Bear,* a song he wrote for his friend Johnny Preston, which was a major hit at the end of 1959. Completing the bill were the rather obscure Frankie Sardo, whose most famous hour this presumably must have been, and the still emerging Dion and the Belmonts, showcasing the song that would become the first of several hits for them. *Teenager In Love,* which entered the American top twenty in May 1959.

Once he had embarked on the tour, Buddy Holly must have been seriously thinking that he had made the wrong decision—although his backing musicians were at least competent, to use a completely new rhythm section was a risk. Holly had chosen Lubbock disc-jockey Waylon Jennings to play bass on the tour, Tommy Allsup on guitar, and a newcomer, Charlie Bunch, completed the group, The New Crickets. Thus, the four-man line up was only temporary, and it seems unlikely that the music they produced was up to the standard Holly had achieved with the Crickets. Another worry must have been Maria Elena, who was pregnant, and was too unwell to accompany her husband on tour.

By the beginning of February 1959, a few days into the tour, the performers were in rather less than perfect condition. Problems with transport, exposure to the cold and lack of sleep combined with apparently poor organisation had left them somewhat bedraggled, and when the tour reached Clear Lake, Iowa, Holly decided that he would have to take some action to ensure that his excellent reputation did not become tarnished either by his appearance (the various delays had resulted in an inability even to do essential laundry) or by his lacklustre performance, which would inevitably occur sooner or later through fatigue. The best plan

One of the last publicity photographs of Buddy.

he could come up with was to charter a private plane to fly himself, Allsup and Jennings to the next stop on the tour—this would enable them to wash their clothes and get some much-needed rest in a conventional bed as opposed to curling up on the seats of the tour bus. It was 400 miles to Moorhead, where the package was next scheduled to perform, and taking a plane might cut the time of the journey by up to six or seven hours.

A plane and pilot were found after some searching. The pilot was Roger Peterson, a young and somewhat inexperienced flyer, who obviously wanted to make the trip, either because he was impressed with the fame of his passengers, or perhaps more likely because he was short of money. The idea was to fly to Fargo, North Dakota, the nearest airport to Moorhead. When Ritchie Valens and the Big Bopper heard about Holly's plan, they separately approached Allsup and Jennings, and persuaded them to give up their places on the aircraft—Valens was as unhappy as the others about the appalling conditions and the Big Bopper had contracted a cold, which was already hampering his performance, and which would not be improved by another night on the bus.

The show that night took place in the Surf Ballroom, by the side of Clear Lake. According to eyewitnesses, Buddy Holly and the Crickets were the best-received act on the bill, in spite of the fact that both the Big Bopper and Ritchie Valens had records in the charts at the time. Before an audience of over 1000, Holly sang most of his single releases, but it is reported that he did not sing his current release *It Doesn't Matter Anymore.* Carroll Anderson, the manager of the Surf Ballroom, chatted with Holly backstage during the show. He asked the young singer how far he expected to go in the music business, and Holly is quoted as saying with a grin: 'Well, I'm either going to go to the top—or else I'm going to fall. But I think you're going to see me in the bigtime.' Holly also rang Maria Elena in New York that evening, but he did not tell her of his intention to fly to the next engagement, probably because he did not want to worry her, knowing she had a fear of small planes. He did however tell her that he was travelling ahead of the others to make arrangements for the show, and when she asked him why he should, he said: 'There's nobody else to do it.'

After the show, Holly, Valens and Richardson were driven to Mason City, Iowa, which was the

VOLUME 90

CLEAR LAKE, IOWA, THURSDAY, FEBRUARY 5, 1959

NUMBER 2

DEATH OF SINGERS HERE SHOCKS NATION

Rock 'n Rollers, Pilot Die in Tragic Plane Crash

There was no fearful omen of tragedy Monday night when 1,100 teenagers and their parents packed the Surf Ballroom in Clear Lake for a gala "rock 'n roll" dance. Featured were four nationally-known entertainers: Buddy Holly and the Crickets; the "Big Bopper"; Ritchie Valens; and Dion and the Belmonts.

The entertainers were full of pep, reacting joyously to the big crowd of young people. The "Big Bopper" (J. P. Richardson), who wrote the hit song "Chantilly Lace," and Ritchie Valens, author of several top hits, playfully Indian wrestled backstage between acts.

Two hours after the dance, three of the four singers were dead, along with the pilot who was flying them to Fargo, N.D., for another appearance. Their broken bodies were found in and around the wreckage of the light plane they had chartered after the dance Monday night.

Dead were the pilot, Roger Peterson, 21, of Clear Lake; Charles (Buddy) Holly, 22, of Lubbock, Texas; Ritchie Valens (Richard Valenzuela), 17, of Los Angeles, Calif.; J. P. (Big Bopper) Richardson, 28, Beaumont, Texas.

Word of their death when the plane was found Tuesday morning in a snow covered field six miles north of the airport focused nationwide attention on Clear Lake. The three singers are considered among the top rock 'n roll artists in the United States and their recordings are currently on the best selling list, some over the million mark.

THE FATAL CRASH occurred on the Albert Juhl farm, in a pasture about a half mile west of the farm house. The plane, a Beechcraft Bonanza chartered from the Dwyer Flying service, took off about 1 a.m. from the airport with the three men after they were taken to the airport by Carroll Anderson, Surf manager, his wife and son, Tommy.

It is believed to have crashed shortly thereafter into the field on the Juhl farm.

WRECKAGE OF THE PLANE was discovered by Jerry Dwyer about 9:30 a.m. Tuesday. He had received no reports from the plane since it departed and he began the search in another plane Tuesday morning.

The craft first scraped the ground at a spot in the middle of the field, breaking off one wing and other parts of the plane.

It then bounced and skidded about 200 yards further to the northwest, scattering wreckage and debris along the way until it piled into a wire fence along the north end of the pasture.

The plane was completely demolished in the crash, but did not burn.

The bodies of the three entertainers were thrown from the plane, two of them lying a short distance to the south of the plane, and the third was thrown over the fence about 20 feet into the next field.

The body of the pilot was entangled amid the wreckage of the main part of the plane. Ambulances took the victims to the Ward and Wilcox Funeral homes in Clear Lake.

An investigation was launched by the Civil Aeronautics administration after the crash to determine its cause. Jerry Dwyer, operator of the flying service, could give no reason, stating that the plane was in good condition and that Mr. Peterson was a competent pilot.

Indications pointed to the fact that the plane touched the ground at a low angle, skidding along the field instead of plunging steeply into the ground. The only mark at the place where it first hit was a furrow scraped out by a wing tip.

CAA INVESTIGATORS arrived in Clear Lake later Tuesday and remained overnight. Guards were posted at the scene throughout the day and through Tuesday night to keep the wreckage intact for the investigation.

The major significance of loss of the three artists to the music world was indicated by the immediate requests of national press associations for full coverage. Requests also have been received from Life magazine for pictures.

Other members of the troupe who appeared at the Surf Monday night were traveling to Fargo by chartered bus.

Ironically, Buddy Holly had told KRIB disc jockey Bob Hale at the Surf that he didn't want to take a chance in the bus since it had broken down while traveling from Green Bay, Wis., to Clear Lake the day before.

The three therefore decided to charter the plane and take care of advance arrangements in Fargo Tuesday.

Valens, who only last year was a high school student at San Fernando, Calif., had just finished his first movie and his song, "Donna" sold more than a million records.

Richardson, known as the "Big Bopper," won nationwide fame for the song, "Chantilly Lace" which he wrote some months ago.

Buddy Holly, singing star of the Crickets, has made eight records, two of which, "Peggy Sue" and "That'll Be the Day," sold over a million and a half copies. His newest record, just released, is "It Doesn't Matter Any More."

• • • • •

ROGER PETERSON was born May 24, 1937, at Alta, the son of Arthur and Pearl Kramer Peterson. He graduated from Fairview Consolidated school in 1954, attended Ross Aviation school at Tulsa, Okla., and was employed by the Graham Flying service at Sioux City, before coming to Clear Lake about a year ago.

He was a member of the Redeemer Lutheran church at Ventura and of the Clear Lake Junior Chamber of Commerce.

Mr. Peterson and De Ann Lenz were married Sept. 14, 1958, in Alta and had resided in Clear Lake since their marriage in one of the Armsbury cottages on N. Shore dr.

Besides his wife, he is survived by his parents; two brothers, Ronald and Robert; one sister, Janet; his grandmother, Mrs. Elmer A. Peterson of Sioux Rapids.

Funeral services were held at 2 p.m. Thursday (today) at the Redeemer Lutheran church with the Rev. E. H. Widmann officiating. Services also will be held at 2 p.m. Friday at St. Paul's Lutheran church at Alta with burial to be in the Storm Lake Memorial cemetery.

Arrangements in Clear Lake were through the Wilcox Funeral home.

THE BODY OF J. P. RICHARDSON was taken by air Wednesday to Beaumont, Texas, for funeral service. He was born Oct. 24, 1930, and is survived by his wife, Adrian, and a daughter, Deborah, who are in New Orleans. Mrs. Richardson also is expecting another child.

Arrangements here were through the Ward Funeral home.

THE BODY OF RITCHIE VALENS was scheduled to be taken by rail Wednesday to San Fernando, Calif., for funeral services.

Richard Valenzuela was born May 13, 1941, to Mr. and Mrs. Joseph Valenzuela. He is survived by his mother, Conception Reyes of Pacoima, Calif. Arrangements for Mr. Valens were completed through the Ward Funeral home.

THE BODY OF CHARLES (BUDDY) HOLLY, who was born Sept. 7, 1936, was taken by plane Wednesday afternoon to Lubbock, Texas, for funeral serv... ments here were completed through ...

BODY OF CRASH VICTIM, one of four killed Monday night north of Clear Lake, lies front of wreckage of light plane. Accident took the lives of three nationally famous rock 'n roll entertainers ...

Latest In Home Improvement ....

Home Show Feb. 19-22

Clear Lake's third annual Home Show, Feb. 19 through 22 will introduce the most modern and latest in equipment and materials for making home improvements and changes, announced Roscoe Miller, president of the local home show association.

According to Miller, the 1959 home show will be even better and larger ... all the space of the Vets Social Center, ... the show again is held, will be used ... plays and exhibits.

... should captivate ... of all household... builders, and the ... since doz... sugges-tions as well as the latest merchandise will be on display, Miller stated.

Prizes valued at several hundred dollars will be given away during the show, including at least two valuable prizes each night, according to Bill Eaton and John Perkins, who are in charge of prizes. The grand award will be a sterophonic hi-fi player system.

The charge for admissions will remain the same, 10 cents, and the proceeds will go to the Junior Chamber of Commerce. The Jaycees will handle the admissions, and the registrations. A lunch and coffee bar, and a rest lounge, will be available for the convenience of all. The Music Mothers will handle the preparations, and even serve complete meals.

One of the features of the show will be a display of small model homes, designed and built to scale by the high school industrial arts class under the direction of James Killam, instructor. The model homes will be judged by a panel of professional home builders for prizes, Miller stated.

Last year, over 3,000 people paid to view the home show, and they represented 80 Iowa communities.

...proval

3 Hospitalized In Rural Crash Tuesday Morning

...ee persons were injured ...-car crash Tuesday ...en it struck a culvert ... north of the ... farm. Taken ... by Ward ... Han... Bak... ...er.

Above:
Buddy's gravestone in Lubbock reverted to the original spelling of his name.

nearest airport serving Clear Lake, and took off during the early hours of February 3rd, 1959. The U.P.I. report gives the take-off time as 1.50 am; John Goldrosen, in his book *Buddy Holly* gives it as being shortly before 1.00 am.

Within minutes of taking off, the four-seater single engine plane crashed on a farm about ten miles from Mason City. The four occupants were killed, cutting short at least one, and possibly three great careers in the rock'n'roll business. The bodies of Buddy Holly and Ritchie Valens lay 20 feet away from the wreckage; J. P. Richardson's body had been thrown 40 feet. They were not discovered until long after dawn, when the owner of the plane, Jerry Dwyer, flew over the same course as Peterson and spotted the remains of the plane. It lay in a cornfield several hundred yards from the nearest farmhouse, but no one had heard the crash. The plane had skidded across the snow and stubble for 558 feet before piling into a wire fence at the north end of the field. The reasons for the crash can only be a matter for conjecture, although the weather conditions, which included light snow and banks of fog, cannot have made Peterson's task easy. To this should be added the fact that Peterson, though a qualified pilot, was not very experienced at instrument flying—and the poor visibility on that night meant that in order to navigate he would have had to rely on the plane's instruments with which he was not familiar. In fact, the Dwyer Flying Service, for whom Peterson was working, was certified for visual flights only. The air traffic communicators at the airport had not informed Peterson of two special weather bureau advisories, which would have alerted him to the fact that he would certainly have to fly by the aid of instruments.

Carroll Anderson, who had arranged the flight, was called out from Clear Lake to identify the bodies. Maria Elena, who had been feeling unwell, was still in bed when she heard the news on the radio. The Holleys heard the news in the same way: 'A light plane has crashed in Iowa. . .' Mrs Holley realised what had happened: 'I knew that the plane flight must have been all Buddy's idea.' Maria Elena tells of strange dreams she and Holly had the night before he left to go on tour, his involving a small plane and separation from Maria Elena, hers involving a ball of fire crashing into the ground in a big, empty prairie.

'I'm either going to go to the top—or else I'm going to fall.'

On Wednesday 4th February, a plane was sent from Texas to bring Buddy Holly's body home to Lubbock, but was unable to return until the following day, owing to the weather conditions. The funeral was held on the afternoon of Saturday 7th February, at the Tabernacle Baptist Church. Over one thousand people, many of them young local fans, attended the ceremony, and tributes were received from all over the world, including a telegram from Elvis Presley, who was at the time stationed in Germany as part of his spell in the U.S. army. The coffin was carried to the grave by Holly's greatest friends in the music business, Jerry Allison, Joe Mauldin, Niki Sullivan, Sonny Curtis, Bob Montgomery and Phil Everly. After less than two years as a rock'n'roll star, Buddy Holly was laid to rest.

The death of popular entertainers during this century has in general resulted in a rather alarming burst of necrophiliac adulation almost immediately after the event, followed by a gradual decrease in

THAT'LL BE THE DAY

Words and Music by

BUDDY HOLLY, NORMAN PETTY and JERRY ALLISON

LAST HOLLY DISCS SOON

THE last unreleased recordings by the late Buddy Holly have now become available and are to be released in this country by Coral in the autumn.

First release is set for Septembe 7. It is Buddy's long-awaited waxir of "Reminiscing," featuring Ki Curtis on sax. An album will issued later.

Some tracks were studio-reco but others feature Buddy Holly's voice and require musical ba which will be added at spec cording sessions in New Mexi month, supervised by manager, Norman Petty.

Petty is currently in Lon pleting details for the Br of this material.

There's no stopping Buddy Holly

Buddy Holly
Reminiscing
Reminiscing; Slippin' And Slidin'; Bo Diddley; Wait Till The Sun Shines, Nellie; Baby, Won't You Please Come Home?; Brown-Eyed Handsome Man; Because I Love You; It's Not My Fault; I'm Gonna Set My Foot Down; Changing All Those Changes; Rock-A-Bye Rock.
(Coral LVA 9212)****

THE phenomenal Buddy Holly story goes on without flagging years after his accidental death, and this LP is a major factor in it.

It's compiled from old tapes in the possession of Buddy's parents, his wife Maria, his recording manager, Norman Petty, and the Coral label people. The Fireballs group have dubbed backings to the songs, and, thanks to Norman Petty and his assistant technical wizards, the results sound like a gen recording session of recent date.

Buddy was a pioneer trail-blazer in the world of ballad beatdom, and this set proves it. You can still hear [illegible] of popsters now putting across their songs with these accents, inflections and mannerisms.

That is Buddy's greatest epitaph. Not only do his fans still put his old tapes into the hit parade time and again, but today's generation of beatsters still pay close attention to his style and ideas.

popularity as the work of the entertainer fades further into the past. Buddy Holly was close to the peak of his popularity at the time of his death, and apparently gaining rather than losing fans. He was the first really big rock'n'roll star to meet an untimely end.

At the time of Buddy Holly's death, his current single release was, as has already been mentioned, *It Doesn't Matter Anymore*; but he is believed never to have played it on stage. On the very day he died, the single entered the top hundred, climbing slowly to peak at number thirteen in America by the end of March 1959. It was to be Holly's final American hit, although a number of other singles have been released subsequently—in fact, it was a double-sided final hit, as *Raining In My Heart,* the B-side of the single, also crept into the chart. Even the rumours circulating America which suggested that flying saucers had been sighted over Lubbock around the time of Buddy's birth were not enough to prevent his popularity going into a rapid decline—perhaps the familiar American trait of refusing to dwell on the past as long as something new and worthwhile exists was being demonstrated. There is nothing so dead as a pop star who is not in the public eye.

In Britain, the story was totally different. *It Doesn't Matter Anymore* was released in haste, ten days after Holly's death, and within two weeks had burst into the chart at number twenty, finally making number one at the end of April, 1959, where it remained for three weeks. Shortly afterwards, an album was compiled under the title *The Buddy Holly Story*, mixing tracks by the Crickets with solo recordings to form a 'Best of' twelve track album, which sold prodigiously for several years in all the countries Buddy had visited, and several more besides. Fresh singles also began to be released on both sides of the Atlantic, although predictably the flow was considerably quicker in Britain than in America. The first of the British posthumous singles was *Midnight Shift/Rock Around With Ollie Vee*, which had not been released as a single before and made the low twenties by July 1959.

After that, the various record companies involved in Holly's career began to look into what Buddy Holly material might exist which they did not know about. The first place to check was with Maria Elena. As a result of the trauma of Buddy's death she had unfortunately lost her baby, but nonetheless she provided the demo tapes of Holly's last six original tracks. Coral Records passed on the tapes to Jack Hansen, one of their house producers, who assembled a group under the name of the Jack Hansen Combo, and under Hansen's control, added what have sometimes been termed 'inappropriate' and 'inadequate' backings. The first product of this posthumous overdubbing came by the end of the summer of 1959, when *Peggy Sue Got Married* and *Crying, Waiting, Hoping* were released back to back as a single. As already noted, extreme apathy was the only reaction in America, although in Britain the record reached to top twenty, and remained in the charts until Christmas.

Hansen had also reprocessed the other four tracks, and these, along with various finished but unreleased masters and a few single B-sides from the previous years, were collected fourteen months after Holly's death under the title of *The Buddy Holly Story Volume 2.* Meanwhile, singles continued to be released in Britain, although the first release of 1960, coupling *Heartbeat* with *Everyday*, was unsuccessful. However, the failure of this single was

Left: Sheet music for 'That'll Be The Day'. Inset: To the music press, Holly's posthumous releases were still news.

In Britain, a constant stream of LPs appeared after Holly's death.

soon forgotten as another previously unheard Holly masterpiece was issued, coupling *True Love Ways* and *Moondreams*.

This single was rather more successful than *Heartbeat,* and briefly entered the British chart. Even twenty years after Buddy's death, two of the people closest to him still cite *True Love Ways* as their favourite Buddy Holly song. Petty probably singles it out because the session which produced the song was the last time that he worked with Holly. Maria Elena's reasons are more intimate. She remembers: 'He used to sing that to me all the time just before he died. It was our secret song.'

Over the next two years, a flurry of singles came out, although for the first time, British releases were not identical to the records Holly's American company put out—by this time, it had been firmly established that there was far more chance of achieving a Buddy Holly hit in Britain. *Learning The Game/That Makes It Tough* was a minor hit at the end of 1960. Holly might not have been too pleased by the posthumous backings that had been provided for the songs, in view of the fact that had he lived, Ray Charles might have been working with him on them. *Learning The Game* was followed during the first half of 1961 by *What To Do/That's What They Say* and *Baby I Don't Care/Valley of Tears,* which were both minor hits, the latter record reaching number fourteen, but nothing was released in America during this period.

By the end of 1961, a constant stream of letters had begun to arrive at the homes and offices of anyone who might have been connected with Holly, requesting, and often demanding, new recordings.

Buddy's acoustic guitar with the leather cover which he made for it.

> **'Buddy would have been unhappy with the fact that his folks went to Norman. But they didn't have any choice if they wanted to keep his name alive.'**

This proof of a continuing demand brought Norman Petty back into the picture, since he was in possession of several unissued tracks by Buddy Holly, such as *Love's Made A Fool Of You, Reminiscing,* and several other demos which had been made at his Clovis studio. Unlike Jack Hansen, who possibly had never met Holly, let alone worked with him, Petty was in a good position to pick up the reins of Holly's career which he had only dropped a few months before the artist's death. However, it seems that slightly more was involved than merely the previous working relationship. Buddy's mother, who had perhaps always been over-protective towards her youngest child, had agreed with Norman Petty in one important respect, that she was unhappy about her son's marriage. While Buddy's father was, and still, is very attached to Maria Elena, Mrs Holley never achieved a similar closeness. As a result, when Petty was able to produce unheard Holly tracks Mrs Holley supported his claims to be the man solely responsible for future Holly recordings. In recent interviews, however, the two have expressed differing opinions when conjecturing about any future Holly/Petty collaboration had the plane crash not occurred. Petty claimed: 'I don't think there ever was a rift between Buddy and I, musically speaking—his parents did say later that they felt Buddy would have liked to come back to Clovis to record.' Ella Holley, on the other hand, said, 'I don't really think they would have gotten together again, but I think their relationship would have been a friendly one. At the time of Buddy's death, they hadn't seen each other for some time, but we (Mr & Mrs Holley) have been special friends with Norman Petty, and we still are.'

During 1962, Petty began to collect from various sources all the unfinished Buddy Holly tracks that he could find. By this time, his relationship with the original Crickets, (Jerry Allison, Joe B. Mauldin and Sonny Curtis), had ended, and the group which Petty had 'discovered' to take their place as his management charges was a four-piece from New Mexico called the Fireballs. Petty used the group to add fresh backing (or in several cases original backings) to the raw demo tapes of Holly he had unearthed. The first tracks to benefit from this process were *Reminiscing* and *Wait Till The Sun Shines Nellie,* which were released together as a single during the autumn of 1962. This was the first American release for over two years, although in Britain, a couple of unsuccessful singles had been issued since *Baby I Don't Care. Reminiscing* reversed that trend, making the top twenty in

10 NEW MUSICAL EXPRESS Friday, April 24, 1959

How I Remember Buddy

...and here is one of many reasons why...

POP ...

DEE-JAY'S TRIBUTE

BUDDY HOLLY

"It Doesn't Matter Anymore"
"Raining In My Heart"

(Coral Q 72360)

★★★★

THIS IS THE RECORD that has leapt into the Top Twenty not only in Britain but in the States as well, following Buddy's untimely death a month ago. As a tribute to "a nice guy and

a first rate performer," America's D.J.'s—who had been letting the disc lie around unplayed before the tragic air-crash — started playing the ironically titled "It Doesn't Matter Anymore".

It was a distinct change of approach for Buddy, for **Dick Jacobs'** backing involved a full orchestra in which the strings play an important rôle. The rhythm is bright and not at all Rock 'n' Roll. Though the mood is bright, the lyrics express a feeling of despondency over a hopeless love.

"Raining In My Heart" opens with strings pizzicato to create the impression of falling rain. Buddy's singing style is distinctive, the orchestration attractive. A very pleasant side.

...r the late Buddy Holly ...s "Peggy Sue," "Rave ...Morning," "That'll Be ...y," "Think It Over" ...'t Matter Any More."

The Crickets toured ... March, I spent a lot of ... Buddy and his col... ...sist Joe B. Mauldin ...r Jerry Allison—and ...se friendship with the ...led rock 'n' roll star. ...ind of friendship that ...rgotten and it has left ...rehouse of memories ...one of the nicest ...ersonalities I've ever ...y was the kind of ...ellow that anybody ...o call a friend. ... a quiet, unaffected ... tastes. He was ... to his many fans ...e him a star and ...is earnest dedica... ...profession.

...wed

...erawed with the ...iness and I'm ... he never fully ...ture and im... ...popular music. **...yed life, and ... for which he ...only anxieties ...uld enjoy his ...t him down.** ...cet of the ...sided per... ...of humour. ...row good ... insults at ... an equal ...n! ... up con... ...after a ...ween the ...t Buddy ...im—the ...e busi... ...t con... ...coach ...nents. ...e fun ...style ...mer... ...the ...un... ...an... ...tle ...ell ...

BUDDY HOLLY appreciated the attention and time that our noted writer, KEITH GOODWIN devoted to him and the other two CRICKETS, when they were in London last year. That's why he wrote on Keith's programme: "Here's our best wishes to the best Press man we have associated with. Best of luck to you, Buddy Holly." Among other things, it is this appreciation, not always given when it is due, that has endeared the memory of Buddy Holly to our Keith.

Says Keith Goodwin

...frivolous sense of humour later that same evening when The Crickets, Norman Petty (their manager) and his ...wife, Vi, Allan Crawford (then ...managing director of Southern Music) ...nd myself returned to the Cumber...nd Hotel for a late supper.

A quiet, dignified waiter approached and the pantomime began. First Joe B. Mauldin ordered, closely followed by Jerry Allison. Between them, they changed their minds about a dozen times—frequently interrupted by exuberant shouts from Buddy as he spotted some new delicacy on the menu.

When Buddy's turn came to order, he chopped and changed his mind—with a winking twinkle in his eyes—so many times that he ended up with no less than four different drinks (non-alcoholic) and a classic assortment of sandwiches before him!

Finally, with the rest of us laughing heartily, Buddy brought the scene to an end with a snappy: "That'll do for a quick snack." Even the waiter saw the joke in the end . . . specially after the big tip Buddy gave him.

But don't let this little incident give the wrong impression that Buddy and his colleagues were ill-mannered or unduly mischievous. On the contrary, they were extremely well-behaved, well-groomed, polite and courteous at all times.

'Doorman'

Back in April, 1958, in our companion monthly publication "Hit Parade," Buddy recounted how The Crickets and I toured London in Allan Crawford's car at two o'clock in the morning inspecting the automobile showrooms. What he didn't tell you was that each time our car stopped, he made a point of being first out to open the doors for us. In short, Buddy was a gentleman.

There's perhaps little need for me to remind you that Buddy was devoted to music.

Rock 'n' roll wasn't the only style he liked, however. He told me once that he enjoyed anything that moved him in some way and was played well.

An incident worth recalling happened after one of the group's Kilburn concerts. While Buddy and the boys were changing, Norman Petty (himself a talented pianist, organist, composer and arranger with a million-seller to his credit in "Almost Paradise") decided to take a look around the vast Gaumont State Cinema.

Impromptu

It was only natural that he should locate the theatre organ and, without thinking, he sat down and idly played a few notes. Buddy came storming out of his dressing room, singing Norman's praises and urging him to play.

There must have been a dozen of us grouped around the organ while Norman played. Even the usherettes and attendants forgot about going home. But no one was more enthusiastic than Buddy.

Then there was the occasion at Walthamstow Granada where, in the dressing room, between shows, I sat in a corner reading through the top twenty U.S. disc hits printed in the NME. Buddy put on an impromptu concert with The Crickets for me, working their way through all the tunes I called out, then unreleased in Britain—they wanted me to have an idea what they were about.

I mention this in order to stress Buddy's dedication to music. On stage or off, he was rarely without his guitar. He practised diligently and was ready to discuss music at the drop of a hat. More important, too—he was always willing to learn.

Farewell

The last time I saw Buddy was at London Airport just a few hours after his final performance at Hammersmith. We made the trip together by car, and I noticed during the journey that the singer appeared a trifle sad now that he was leaving a strange country he had grown to love.

Before he stepped out on to the tarmac, Buddy turned, gripped my hand, and drawled lazily: "Well, Keith, that's about it. It's been fun and I'm sure glad you've been around. Take care, now, and I'll see you next year."

I did take care. Buddy did, too. But fate wasn't on his side. And although the words of the song say it doesn't matter any more, I can assure you that to me, it does—very much.

Tributes and reviews continued to be written.

Britain, and was enough to allow Petty to establish himself as the right man to supervise the remaining Buddy Holly material.

Using the Fireballs to copy and occasionally invent backings, Petty put together the first LP assembled under this arrangement, which was also called *Reminiscing*. The album contained a bewildering mixture of tracks without a trace of chronology — some, like an alternative version of *I'm Changing All Those Changes,* had been recorded before the Crickets were formed, while others, like the slow version of *Slippin' and Slidin',* were from the final series of home demos which Maria Elena had been advised to hand over to Petty, despite her misgivings about him. The results, if a little schizophrenic due to the variety of recording locations and dates, were quite successful.

Why did Petty not use Jerry Allison and Joe Mauldin to help him? They were still around Lubbock, and as Holly's best friends and musical associates, must have been able to contribute a great deal more than the Fireballs. Jerry Allison in particular has been critical of the way in which his original drum parts were wiped from the demo tapes and replaced by the Fireballs: 'He had them play on songs that just didn't need anything extra, songs like *Brown Eyed Handsome Man* and *Bo Diddley.*' These were the first two Holly releases of 1963, and both became British top ten hits. It was certainly not his intention to denigrate the playing of the Fireballs, but rather Norman Petty's erasure of all his connections with the songs from the tapes.

By the end of 1963, Petty had assembled another album's worth of tracks, although some of the material he used was sufficiently complete to reduce the need for overdubbing to a minimum. *Love's Made A Fool Of You,* for example, was a completed demo, and *Come Back Baby* had originated from the King Curtis session, although many of the other tracks were taken from various home tapes. *Rock Round With Ollie Vee,* which was also included, predated the Crickets, of course, creating another chronological nightmare. The album was released under the title *Showcase* during the first half of 1964. By this time, the potential for further Buddy Holly hits, even in Britain, had all but dissipated, and only *Wishing*, the other track recorded at the *Love's Made A Fool Of You* session, was left as an original hit single, reaching number twelve during September 1963. After that time, practically every track released on either side of a 45 was available somewhere previously in album form, so perhaps the subsequent lack of single hits is no great surprise.

The next source of material to which Petty turned was Holly's very earliest recordings made with Bob Montgomery, and for the first time, the British and American track listings of an album were not identical. The American version of *Holly In The Hills* contained eight tracks with participation by Bob Montgomery, fleshed out with a couple of Crickets' B-sides, *What To Do* from the final New York home tapes, and *Wishing*. The British version, although having the same title of *Holly In The Hills,* included all eleven early tracks with Montgomery, with the addition of *Wishing,* which was co-written by Montgomery, and had also been a hit. Once again, the Fireballs were called in to 'beef up' the original tapes.

After *Holly In The Hills,* a long gap occurred before any further original Holly material was allowed to escape, although a number of compilation albums were released at various times on both sides of the Atlantic. In Britain, each new LP which came out during the first half of the sixties made a significant chart impact, even the collection of pre-Crickets Decca material, which was sneakily released under the title of *That'll Be The Day,* an early inferior version of the song packaged with a number of other tracks. In America, a double album titled *The Best Of Buddy Holly* came out in 1966, and in the succeeding year, both Britain and America released a *Great Hits* LP, although the track selections were dissimilar.

In 1968, six of the possible eight Holly albums, the exceptions being *That'll Be The Day* and *The 'Chirping' Crickets,* were released as a matching series. Each of the six sleeves carried an identical cartoon of Buddy, superimposed on a different pastel-coloured background. The albums were given new titles—*Buddy Holly,* for example, became *Listen To Me,* and *The Buddy Holly Story* was retitled *Rave On.* Shortly afterwards, both the albums not included in the matching repackage were released on a budget label, a second *Greatest Hits* album was compiled, and amid the excitement, a single reissue of *Peggy Sue/Rave On* entered the top thirty for a week. And this was more than nine years after Buddy Holly had died....

By 1969, the tenth anniversary of Buddy's death, the ground beneath the barrel was being scraped, and Petty came up with a ten track album titled *Giant,* which more or less meant that he had come to the end of the possibilities for 'new' material. Predictably, the LP was another curious mixture. The quality of the majority of the released recording is less than acceptable, and had the album been the work of anyone other than Holly or perhaps Elvis Presley, it seems highly unlikely that it would have been released. In Britain, of course, it made the chart for a short time, continuing proof of the British dedication of their hero.

Below: A gold disc for UK sales of '20 Golden Greats' is presented to Maria Elena by Ralph Witsell of MCA (left). John Beecher, the foremost authority on Holly, is on the right.

Subsequent to *Giant,* the only item of any interest to have emerged other than the occasional alternate (and practically indistinguishable) version of some well known track, was a 1971 LP released only in Britain under the title *Remember.* This contained several tracks which had not appeared in album form before, like *Lonesome Tears* and *Fool's Paradise,* along with Jerry Allison's *Real Wild Child,* and a few previously unheard tracks like *That's My Desire* (from the *Rave On* session) and an early version of *Maybe Baby.* The album was completed by the final six tracks written and recorded by Holly just before he died, with fresh Fireballs overdubs. The situation had reached the stage where one set of posthumous backings were replaced by another. Other than that, little new material has surfaced, perhaps the most interesting item being the release for the first time in 1975 of the alternate version of *Rock Around With Ollie Vee* on the umpteenth repackage of the early Decca material under the title of *The Nashville Sessions.* As far as can be ascertained, the recorded catalogue of Buddy Holly's work has now been exhausted. But the market is still there—and this is amply demonstrated by MCA's twentieth anniversary issue of a boxed six-album set of everything ever attributed to Buddy Holly—called *The Complete Buddy Holly.*

The Legacy Of Buddy Holly

CHAPTER FIVE

Buddy Holly's posthumous impact on the history of popular music began literally at once, and has continued unabated ever since. The first singer to be directly influenced by his death was Robert Velline, otherwise known as Bobby Vee. Aged only seventeen at the time, Bobby Vee's career began on the day after the plane crash. He had been looking forward to seeing Holly play that night in Moorhead, Minnesota, but of course his hopes were dashed. However, in best show business tradition, it was decided that the show must go on and auditions were held in Moorhead for local musicians to fill the gaps on the bill. The winner was Bobby Vee. Backed by his brother's group, Bobby sang half a dozen Holly songs so successfully that he was signed up by United Artists Records. In succeeding years, he became a major factor in keeping Buddy Holly's music alive. While his talent may not have been the equal of Holly's, his 'teen dream' appearance allowed him to retain his popularity throughout most of the sixties. However, it wasn't until late 1960 that a Vee cover of a Holly song was released. *Everyday* was issued as the B-side of *Rubber Ball,* a top ten hit on both sides of the Atlantic.

Vee's most obvious tribute to Buddy Holly came later, in the form of an album titled *I Remember Buddy Holly,* which contains eleven very reasonable cover versions of Holly's best known recordings, plus a track called *Buddy's Song,* the lyrics of which are almost totally composed of song titles associated with Holly. Even before he recorded the Holly tribute LP, Bobby Vee had made another album with Holly associations, *Bobby Vee Meets The Crickets,* which included versions of *Peggy Sue, Bo Diddley* and *Well . . . All Right,* along with other fifties rock standards.

The first real 'tribute' record to come after Holly's death was *Three Stars,* recorded by a disc jockey in San Bernadino, California, named Tommy Dee. Dee had written the song in his car in twenty minutes flat immediately after hearing the news of the crash. 'I had never met Buddy,' he said recently, 'I sort of felt that the type of guy he was was a shy and bashful type of guy just from looking at his picture. I guess it kinda seems I hit the nail on the head.' Even though it may have emerged that Buddy was not as bashful as many people thought, this was certainly the way the fans wanted to remember him. The song sold about 6 million copies in its various versions, which included one cut by Eddie Cochran. Cochran was so moved by the song which he recorded the evening after the crash that he started crying, and it took three takes to record. 'He really couldn't get it, he broke up so much,' said Dee. 'He knew the artists so well, and they were such good friends.' Liberty Records, Cochran's recording company, did not release his version until after Cochran's own tragic death in a car accident in Britain in 1959.

But it was the continuing saga of cover versions of songs written by and/or associated with Holly that really kept his name in the public eye after his death. Of less than a hundred songs recorded by Buddy Holly, more than twenty have been covered by notable artists. *Everyday* which was a B-side when Holly first released it, has probably been used

Left: The Crickets in London in 1977. L. to r.: Sonny Curtis, Joe B. Mauldin and Jerry Allison. Below: Eddie Cochran recorded a tribute to the trio killed in February 1959, with the title 'Three Stars'. Tragically, Cochran was himself killed in April 1960.

Linda Ronstadt has successfully recorded several Holly songs.

more than any of the other songs, among the more notable versions being those by John Denver, Don McLean and Phillip Goodhand-Tait. Another of the lesser-known Holly songs, *It's So Easy,* has also attracted a number of covers, from the country music versions by Waylon Jennings and Skeeter Davis to the more mainstream styling of Linda Ronstadt, who achieved a top ten hit with the song in 1977.

In some cases, the list of those who have recorded a Holly song is impressive in its very diversity—*Love's Made A Fool Of You,* for instance, was recorded by the Crickets after they had left Buddy Holly, and there have been hit versions of the song by hard rockers the Bobby Fuller Four, and English country rockers Cochise, as well as Tom Rush and British folk/rock stars Sandy Denny and Richard Thompson.

That'll Be The Day is another much used title—having been covered by the Everly Brothers, Francoise Hardy, Pat Boone and Linda Ronstadt, the last version being a 1976 top twenty hit. David Essex starred in Ray Connolly's film *That'll Be The Day* (1972), which was a nostalgic look back at life in Britain during the late fifties and early sixties. There have been more than a dozen cover versions, too, of *Oh Boy!* In addition, in the late fifties one of the first British TV rock shows was also entitled *Oh Boy!* by its enthusiastic producer, Jack Good. It frequently featured artists like Cliff Richard and Marty Wilde singing Holly songs and the final edition ended with Cliff, Marty and Billy Fury each singing a verse of *Early In The Morning.* Twenty years later, in 1979, Jack Good has been able to

Elvis Costello also uses Holly's trademark glasses.

revive *Oh Boy!* as a rock'n'roll stage show.

A number of successful acts and artists have used Buddy Holly songs as their first step on the ladder of hits. One of the best known groups is the Rolling Stones, whose first top ten record in 1964 was a rearrangement of *Not Fade Away*, acknowledging their debt to both Buddy Holly and Bo Diddley. The song was recently quoted by Buddy's mother as being her favourite amongst the songs associated with her son.

There are also connections between the Beatles and Buddy Holly. The Beatles copied *Words of Love* very accurately on their *Beatles For Sale* LP and Paul McCartney has been a long time admirer. Roy Orbison once described the Beatles as being 'just like Buddy Holly and the Crickets but louder'.

Both John Lennon and Paul McCartney have indicated their continuing affection for Holly's music during the seventies, although in different ways. When John Lennon made his *Rock'n'Roll* album, produced by Phil Spector, among the songs he recorded was *Peggy Sue.* Paul McCartney's interest is rather more concrete. During the latter part of the seventies, his company, MPL Productions, has actually acquired the publishing rights to the majority of Buddy Holly's compositions. McCartney's father-in-law and business adviser, Lee Eastman, apparently suggested to him that it might be a useful business move to acquire a song catalogue, at which McCartney immediately mentioned Buddy Holly's. At the time of writing, MPL own all the songs written by Holly under Norman Petty's aegis, since Southern Music and Norman Petty both sold their American rights to McCartney, although Southern Music still own 50% of the publishing in Britain. This represents all Holly's own compositions with the exception of the songs he wrote in New York shortly before his death.

One of the reasons why Lee Eastman was no doubt content that MPL should own the Holly catalogue is that the songs continue to collect cover versions. *Rave On,* for example, has been recorded by Marty Wilde, Waylon Jennings, the Nitty Gritty Dirt Band, and the Outlaws, while *Well... All Right,* has been covered by pop artists like Bobby Sherman, country singers like Skeeter Davis and progressive groups like the short-lived Eric Clapton/Stevie Winwood collaboration, Blind Faith (the world's first supergroup) and the Latin American rhythm dominated Santana. *It Doesn't Matter Anymore* substantially helped in the rejuvenation of Linda Ronstadt's career when she recorded it in 1975. *I'm Gonna Love You Too* (recorded by Blondie) and *Crying, Waiting, Hoping* (by Wreckless Eric) proved that Buddy Holly's material is even suitable recording material for late seventies' New Wave artists, and Leo Sayer scored a massive hit in late 1978 with *Raining In My Heart.* It seems that whatever anyone may feel about Buddy Holly, his peers and their successors in rock'n'roll have never forgotten his brilliant records—it has even been suggested recently that one of the best known songs written by Elvis Costello, *Alison,* may actually be a subtle tribute to

Wreckless Eric cut a New Wave version of 'Crying, Waiting, Hoping'.

Buddy Holly, using the name of Holly's drummer. This may seem a little far-fetched, although it is certainly true that Costello, like Elton John before him, is able to justify his bespectacled appearance by pointing out that one of the biggest stars of all time, Buddy Holly, also wore glasses, and it did not affect his appeal.

But what happened to the Crickets? At the time of Buddy Holly's death, they had opted to remain with Norman Petty, having been convinced that the name of the Crickets was far better known than that of Buddy Holly. The theory was that Buddy Holly was to be replaced by another singer/guitarist, vocalist Earl Sinks, who had previously worked in a band with Tommy Allsup. But Sinks was not a sufficiently capable guitarist to replace both facets of Holly, so Sonny Curtis was asked to rejoin. Even before Christmas 1958, this new formation had gone into Norman Petty's Clovis studio to cut two tracks for their first single without Buddy Holly, *Love's Made A Fool Of You* and *Someone, Someone.*

Unfortunately, the single was unable to qualify as a chart contender, whereupon the Crickets decided to split with Norman Petty. Their failure without Buddy must have led them to think that they had made the wrong decision when opting to remain under Petty's control. In fact, they had telephoned Maria Elena in New York shortly after Buddy left to work on the fateful tour. Maria reported that there was no trace of animosity in the conversation—'They laughed, and they told me they wanted to get back together with Buddy.' Perhaps they were beginning to realize that Maria Elena may have been correct in her suspicions.

The Crickets made arrangements with Coral Records to record in New York during May and

Joe Ely, Lubbock's second most famous musician.

June, 1959. They were to work with Jack Hansen as producer, who by this time was beginning to produce backings for the final six Holly tracks, and perhaps appreciated any assistance that Jerry Allison could give as to how Holly might have arranged his songs. At least half a dozen tracks were cut during this period, including Curtis' classic 'punk' song, *I Fought The Law (and the law won).*

The Crickets' New York recordings were no more successful commercially than those made in Clovis. By the end of 1959, the group had decided to move to Los Angeles, which was just beginning to assume its current significance in the world of rock'n'roll. During November 1959, the group cut their first tracks on the West Coast under the production control of Bud Dant. Included were versions of rock'n'roll classics like Huey Smith's *Rockin' Pneumonia and the Boogie Woogie Flu* and Jerry Lee Lewis' *Great Balls Of Fire,* but still the group were unsuccessful. It was at this point that Earl Sinks left the group, allowing Sonny Curtis to assume the role of lead singer. This move, however, was not to be permanent, as Curtis was called up for national service in the U.S. Army during the first part of 1960, and was away from the group for two years. However, before Uncle Sam forced his unwelcome affections on him, Curtis was able to make two of the very best post-Holly Crickets recordings, *Baby My Heart* and *More Than I Can Say.*

Allison and Mauldin remained in California during 1960, recruiting singer/guitarist David Box and another guitarist, Ernie Hall, to replace Curtis, and in this formation, made two more tracks for Coral, one of which was Holly's *Peggy Sue Got Married,* before group and record company mutually decided that further collaboration would not be beneficial. By this time, on the strength of his work with Holly and on his own account with the Crickets, Jerry Allison had become a respected and popular session drummer, who often worked backing other artists with Tommy Allsup. Allsup was at one point inveigled by Norman Petty into making a Petty – produced album titled *The Buddy Holly Songbook*, and the two ex-Crickets found themselves frequently working for Liberty/United Artists Records. Thus, when the Coral contract came to an end, Allison was happy to sign the Crickets to Liberty Records. Joe B. Mauldin had by this time decided that he was less interested in performing, eventually becoming a successful recording engineer in California, where he remained for some time until moving to Nashville, where he co-owns his own studio.

With Liberty, the Crickets were far more successful than they had been with Coral. Various members joined and left the group, the only constant factors being Jerry Allison, and, on his return from military service, Sonny Curtis.

The peculiar syndrome whereby America was far behind Britain in appreciation of music by Buddy Holly was echoed in the response to the Crickets. The group toured Britain with some success on a number of occasions during the first half of the sixties, and scored two hits for Liberty Records with *Don't Ever Change,* a song written by the hitmaking team of Gerry Goffin and Carole King, and *My Little Girl,* a Sonny Curtis song which was also featured in an atrocious British rock film, *Just For Fun*, made in 1963. But by the mid-sixties, the Crickets were to all intents and purposes past their hit making days.

By 1970, Allison and Curtis seemed to have gone to ground; they appeared on an eponymous LP by

Jerry Allison, Paul McCartney and Joe B. Mauldin during the 1977 Buddy Holly Week in London.

Rolling Stones Ron Wood (left) and Mick Jagger, Tony Barrett (president of the Eddie Cochran Fan Club) and Paul McCartney were among the appreciative audience for the Crickets' concert during the 1977 Buddy Holly Week.

Eric Clapton, which also featured such stars of the era as Delaney and Bonnie, Rita Coolidge, and Allison's old friend Leon Russell. This presumably led to the making of a new Crickets LP in 1971, under the title *Rockin' Fifties Rock'n'Roll,* which was released on Andy Williams' Barnaby label, and featured Curtis, Allison and Glen D. Hardin, (a Cricket recruited for a while in the early sixties), playing a series of predominantly Buddy Holly songs. By 1972, there was apparently sufficient demand for the group to play in Britain again, so the Crickets reformed for a tour and invited English bass player Rick Grech to join them. For the first time the Crickets tried to come to terms with a more modern style of music, mixing rock'n'roll oldies with newer songs, and this updating was also reflected in two subsequent albums, only one of which was fully released, which also used the formidable talents of British guitarist Albert Lee.

When Paul McCartney's MPL Productions acquired the Buddy Holly publishing catalogue, it was decided that an annual Buddy Holly Week should occur each September in London around Buddy's birthday. The first of these occasions, in 1976, was marked by a visit to Britain by Norman Petty for a commemorative lunch and a dance at London's Lyceum Ballroom with a Buddy Holly disco. In 1977, the Crickets reformed specially to play a concert in London. The group was composed of Jerry Allison, Sonny Curtis and Joe B. Mauldin, who was persuaded to come out of bass playing retirement for the occasion. The group had not played together in this form before an audience since 1960, and were watched by an enthusiastic crowd which included Mick Jagger and Ronnie Wood of the Rolling Stones. The experience also led to the Crickets recording again. In May 1978, the reformed trio cut two songs in Joe B. Mauldin's Nashville studio, a fresh version of *Rock Around With Ollie Vee* and a Jerry Allison song, *Cruise In It.* The single was co-produced by John Beecher, perhaps the world's foremost Buddy Holly/Crickets fan and *aficionado*, and was released on his Roller-coaster label.

The 1978 Buddy Holly Week was climaxed by a midnight showing of the film, *The Buddy Holly Story,* and was attended by numerous present day stars who were also long-standing Holly fans, including Keith Moon of the Who, who unfor-

Don McLean, whose hit 'American Pie' commemorated Holly's death.

tunately died the next day. It is intended that the annual Buddy Holly week should be continued as long as there is interest from the public, which seems likely for years to come.

Another aspect of the McCartney involvement with Buddy Holly relates to an album made by McCartney's colleague in Wings, Denny Laine, titled *Holly Days.* The LP completely consists of Buddy Holly songs sung and played by Denny, Paul and his wife, Linda. Of course, to record an entire LP of Holly songs was not a new idea—apart from the records by Bobbie Vee and Tommy Allsup already mentioned, Jimmy Gilmer recorded an album under the title of *Buddy's Buddy,* a peculiar sentiment particularly when it is believed that Holly and Gilmer never actually met, while an obscure group called New York Public Library made an album titled *Raw Holly* a few years ago.

The influence of the Holly heritage often occurs in the strangest places. For example British record producer Joe Meek, who scored numerous hits with the Tornados, the Honeycombs and other mid-sixties British artists, was a diehard Holly freak. He is said to have arranged seances in an attempt to contact Holly after his death. It is surely no coincidence that Meek committed suicide on the eighth anniversary of Buddy's death. One of the artists in Meek's stable was songwriter Geoff Goddard, who penned several hits during the sixties. One of the most interesting was *Tribute to Buddy Holly*, which Meek produced for singer Mike Berry, and which was a hit, also creating a connection between Berry and Buddy Holly which has continued to the present day. At the start of 1979, Berry reaffirmed his Holly fixation and recorded the one song of which no Holly recording exists, *Stay Close To Me.*

Historically, Britain has been far ahead of America in its appreciation of Buddy Holly, but during the seventies, there has been an upsurge of interest among his fellow Americans. For example, a music magazine is published in Dallas, Texas, titled *Buddy,* which, although it is not entirely composed of Holly memories and trivia, frequently refers to him. Another comparatively recent innovation has been the formation in America of the Buddy Holly Memorial Society, which held its first convention (the first ever held in America) in August 1978. One of the Society's executive board members, Joan Turner, has constructed a shrine to Buddy in her home, containing obvious items like records and newspaper cuttings, but also with personal ephemera including letters written by Holly. Even Waylon Jennings, who refused to answer questions about Buddy Holly for many years, has returned to his roots by including on his 1978 LP, *I've Always Been Crazy*, a medley of Buddy Holly hits on which he is backed by the Crickets. By far the most detailed biography of Buddy was written by an American, John Goldrosen, who researched the book for two years, and of course *The Buddy Holly Story* is an American film.

The final confirmation of the almost eternal quality of Buddy Holly's work, a confirmation which effectively silenced any doubters, came with the release in 1978 by MCA Records, of *Buddy Holly Lives: 20 Golden Greats* by Buddy Holly and the Crickets. The album was advertised on television, and garnered vast sales. Many of those who discovered Buddy Holly through this promotion weren't even born when he died.

The definitive recorded epitaph of Buddy Holly has been assembled in 1979 for the twentieth anniversary of his death by John Beecher and fellow Holly expert Malcolm Jones in the form of a six album boxed set titled *The Complete Buddy Holly,* which contains every track Buddy ever recorded, plus the singles he made with Ivan, Waylon Jennings and Lou Giordano and several radio interviews. *The Complete Buddy Holly* is the first complete package ever released of this extraordinary young man's musical testament.

Certainly, no other artist has ever achieved as much in death as Buddy. Along with Elvis Presley, who had many more years of life to create his legend, Holly is by far the best remembered artist from the fifties, and his death is still commemorated in the media each February. Holly and Presley represent nowadays two sides of the same coin and the nostalgia for the innocent first days of rock'n'roll captured in Don McLean's *American Pie* continues to pull in the fans.

Top: Memorabilia from the seventies. Bottom: Allison and Mauldin with MCA employees Martin Sutterthwaite and Jimmy Bowen, at the presentation of gold discs for '20 Golden Greats'.

The ZOO's
Buddy
The Original Texas Music Magazine
THE BUDDY HOLLY MEMORIAL ISSUE
Buddy Holly
★ HIS WIDOW SPEAKS
★ DALLAS TOP HOLLY FAN
★ NEW MOVIE ABOUT THE LEGEND
★ TOP STARS COMMENT ON BUDDY
KZEW

BUDDY FREE
THE ORIGINAL TEXAS MUSIC MAGAZINE FEBRUARY, 1974
Rock & Roll

BUDDY HOLLY LIVES
BUDDY HOLLY LIVES

The Movie

CHAPTER SIX

Considering the vast range of topics which have become vehicles for celluloid entertainment, and the formulae which have led them to be successful, it becomes clear that the life of Buddy Holly would be an ideal cinematic subject. Holly's life was, after all, the perfect tale of the underdog conquering the system until he meets an accidental end. Apart from that, the elements of romance in the story of this all-American hero, coupled with its crucial involvement with rock'n'roll music (the entertainment medium which is the only serious rival to television) make it the perfect commodity for the box office. But it has been nearly twenty years since the death of Holly before a film about his life has been completed. This film is *The Buddy Holly Story,* produced by Ed Cohen and Fred Bauer, and directed by Steve Rash.

It wasn't until 1973 that the first attempt to film Buddy Holly's life story was made. There seems to be no particular reason for such tardiness, other than the waning of interest in Holly's music in his native land. But the 1970s have seen a resurgence of interest in fifties' culture generally, and the enormous success of films like *That'll Be The Day* in Britain and *American Graffiti* in America firmly established a market for rock'n'roll nostalgia.

The first company to express an interest in a Buddy Holly film was ABC-TV, who intended to make the project part of a series of TV 'Movies of the Week', but were unable to convince enough of the surviving characters who were to be portrayed in the film to give their permission for such a project. It must have been around the same time that Universal Pictures began to consider something similar, for which they had the assistance of Norman Petty, but all their three separate attempts to acquire rights to the story of Buddy's life were finally frustrated.

Left: Gary Busey stars in the title role of 'The Buddy Holly Story'. Below: The opening scene in the roller skating rink from the movie, 'The Buddy Holly Story'.

The nearest anyone came to putting the story on film before 1978 was a project entitled *Not Fade Away,* a screen adaptation to be directed by Jerry Friedman of a short memoir by Jerry Allison, concerning a ten day tour which the Crickets (with Buddy) undertook in America's deep south during which they were the only white act on the bill. 20th Century Fox, who financed the idea, actually undertook two weeks of filming in Texas before abandoning the attempt. Different reasons have been postulated for their decision, including difficulties with the acquisition of rights to the story, but the real problem probably concerned the plot. Jerry Friedman told *Rolling Stone* magazine that the film was shut down because of the racialist nature of the script. Jerry Allison recently added, 'I think the first footage showed a lot of hassles with blacks—but then we did get in a lot of hassles with the black guys on the bus.'

It seems that 20th Century Fox were not prepared to risk a furore on the subject of black/white relationships even though the script for the film was apparently very close to fact. According to latter-day Lubbock singer Joe Ely, who auditioned for the lead role in the film, the scenario showed the Crickets, who had top billing on the tour, suffering from a lack of acclaim from the predominantly black audiences and arriving at a point where they had decided to 'buy themselves off the tour'. This ties in with the Crickets' experience on their first tours on America's east coast.

Tommy Allsup has recently confirmed the existence of racial tension on such tours: 'Seems like every damn tour we went on, there would be

eighteen acts, and we'd be the only white act. They were bad back east. Those groups hated us—one time we went into Norfolk, Virginia, and they still couldn't stay in a white hotel. There were about six white acts, and the bus would drop them off and take the black acts to across the tracks to some old funky-ass place. I don't blame them for being pissed off—but they really hated us. The good groups we got along with were like Little Richard—he was great—and Fats Domino, but it was them asshole groups like Little Anthony and the Imperials or the Olympics. The Coasters were good—a couple of them are from Texas—but Lavern Baker, she was a bitch. She took Paul Anka's clothes off him one night in Chicago and covered him with Vaseline, then popped a pillow and put feathers all over him and locked him out in the hallway.' If such events were to be portrayed in *Not Fade Away*, perhaps it's no surprise that it didn't get far past the drawing board.

By the time that executive producer Ed Cohen, director Steve Rash, and producer Fred Bauer joined together in their successful attempt to make a film out of Buddy Holly's life, most, if not all, of the other unsuccessful attempts had fizzled out, although some time earlier, Fred Bauer had approached Jerry Allison to discover whether there was any possibility of sharing the rights of Allison's story with Fox. Although nothing came of that enquiry at the time, Bauer was quite obviously showing an interest several years before the successful project was under way. However, the previous problems experienced with the unsuccessful projects led both Norman Petty and the Crickets to refuse to allow themselves to be portrayed in the Cohen/Rash/Bauer film, which led to severe strains on the plot. The reason for Norman Petty's non-participation in the film is more probably because the script was originally based on John Goldrosen's biography of Buddy Holly, and it is no secret that Goldrosen regarded Petty in many ways as the villain of the Buddy Holly story.

The Buddy Holly Story opens with Buddy Holly as a small town musician playing with a two-piece rhythm section in a roller skating rink. The two players suddenly change their output from bland country and western standards to a roaring version of *Rock Around With Ollie Vee* which immediately transforms their wheel-footed audience from vague apathy to intense enthusiasm. There is also an early romance for Holly, which is based on Buddy's teenage relationship with Echo. In the film, it suggested that she was expecting Buddy to give up his 'flirtation' with popular music, and enter the Baptist ministry, and according to Buddy's mother, there may have been some truth in this. Echo is renamed 'Cindy Lou' for the film and portrayed (by Amy Johnston) as the archetypal 'heavy' girlfriend.

The roles of the two pseudo-Crickets have also been adapted to fit the requirements of the film's plot—Jerry Allison has been renamed Jesse, and is made to seem quite aggressive—while bass player 'Ray Bob' is modelled on Joe B. Mauldin. The scene in the film depicting Holly's first formal recording session in Nashville is full of deviations from the real story—Mauldin was definitely not involved in the Nashville sessions, while a scene which shows Holly becoming uncharacteristically violent towards the producer of the sessions (in real life, Owen Bradley) seems to have little basis in fact. When asked if such a scenario ever occurred Bradley was unable to recall anything of it. Omitting Norman Petty altogether certainly simplifies Holly's career. Rather than having any managerial push behind it, the plot of the film indicates that the recordings of *That'll Be The Day* becomes a hit after a lunatic disc jockey in Buffalo, New York, comes across a tape of the song by chance and plays it non-stop for several days until Holly and the Crickets arrived in New York.

Left and inset: Don Stroud, Gary Busey and Charles Martin Smith re-create a recording session for the film 'The Buddy Holly Story'.

Gary Busey as Buddy Holly, with Amy Johnston as Cindy Lou in 'The Buddy Holly Story'.

The film takes further 'dramatic licence' with Buddy's religious involvement. An early scene set in Holly's local Baptist church shows the preacher condemning rock'n'roll music as an instrument of the devil, leading to the implication that Buddy came into conflict with his religious mentors over his chosen career. But this was far from the truth. Buddy remained on friendly terms with his preacher even after he had achieved fame. It has even been suggested that, in accordance with Baptist practice, Holly donated a percentage of his earnings to the church but that Norman Petty was responsible for diverting the funds from their rightful destination. To remove Norman Petty completely from the film does make clerical indignation more reasonable, since it puts the onus for non-payment onto Buddy Holly himself, but it does seriously distort his relationship with the church.

The film becomes more accurate when Maria Elena is introduced. This comes as no great sur-

'Sign here boys, and you'll be rich.' New York record executive Ross Turner (Conrad Janis) toasts the 'Crickets' in 'The Buddy Holly Story' movie.

prise when it is learned that the producers applied for permission to make the film from Buddy's now remarried widow, and far greater accuracy and depth is thus accorded to the last few months of Holly's life. In particular, the scene where Buddy convinces Maria Elena's aunt that he should be allowed to take Maria out to dinner is well-observed. However, there are still missing items and differences from actual fact in this latter section of the film—for example, Holly is accompanied by an orchestra on the fatal tour, rather than by a Crickets-style backing group. As Norman Petty noted, 'the film-makers forgot, or they didn't know, that Buddy was initially opposed to recording with strings—I had to talk him into it'. There is also a scene showing Holly writing arrangements for a recording session, which is at best unlikely—although Holly could read music, his knowledge of notation was probably rudimentary and could not have run to orchestral arrangements.

The Holley family, too, were disappointed by the film. A scene in which Mr and Mrs Holley are depicted telling Buddy that he should forget about rock'n'roll and take up a respectable trade, is quite without foundation. Mrs Holley, talking to *Rolling Stone* magazine, said 'We were behind Buddy one hundred per cent. We were very anxious for him to make a career as a singer, and we were his biggest fans. The people who made this movie were supposed to consult with us, but we never saw the script at all. It just didn't seem to be the story of Buddy's life, not to anybody who knew him.' Larry Holley, Buddy's brother, was more emphatic: 'It didn't portray his life at all—they didn't ask us about anything, and it was mostly Maria Elena's version of his life, so I didn't feel that was my brother up there on the screen. We weren't happy with the movie at all.' Even Norman Petty was moved to defend the Holley family against their portrayal in the film: 'I was disappointed, because, in my book, Buddy's father is the real hero of the Buddy Holly story. He was the man who gave Buddy this tremendous strength, and Buddy knew he had his father's backing on everything he did—the picture doesn't show the help his father gave Buddy. It makes the Holleys seem like some sort of religious zealots.'

These comments, of course, were only made after the film had been completed. Putting together a script which was acceptable to all those whose permission was needed was obviously a problem, and it seems that scriptwriter Robert Gittler had to make several exhaustive re-writes before it was felt that everyone featured in the film was happy with the way they were portrayed, and that characterisations of those who would not give their permission were sufficiently vague to prevent a spate of lawsuits. Even so, Jerry Allison and Joe B. Mauldin, took out a lawsuit over the use of the Crickets' name. Jerry Allison said, 'They claimed that they were portraying two Crickets from the twelve

Above: In the film of 'The Buddy Holly Story' Buddy (Gary Busey) says goodbye to Marie Elena (played by newcomer Maria Richwine) and below, Busey, although not physically similar to Buddy Holly, is convincing in his film portrayal of the star.

Crickets that there had been, but there weren't twelve Crickets during Buddy's career—there was Niki Sullivan, Joe Mauldin and I.' Possibly, Tommy Allsup, who joined the group virtually as Sullivan's replacement might also have been considered a Cricket, but other than that, it seems that Allison must be correct. Sonny Curtis and Don Guess were members of the Three Tunes, but weren't Crickets in Buddy Holly's time, and neither would Waylon Jennings have considered himself part of the group. In Allison's view the film was 'a tinsel town movie. The shame is that everyone thinks it's true'.

There are, of course, two sides to every story, and the inaccuracies are no worse than those included in most Hollywood 'biopics', and the producers and director were consciously seeking to revitalize the Buddy Holly legend. Ed Cohen claimed, 'We weren't out to hurt anybody, we were just out to make a movie that would make a lot of money, both for us, and for Maria Elena and the Holley family. And I can understand how Mrs Holley feels about the script.' Fred Bauer added, 'We tried to make a commercial film and still be true to what we told Maria Elena and Mr and Mrs Holley, that we were going to make Buddy an American hero.' After all, as Ed Cohen rightly points out, 'There isn't a kid in the entire world who hasn't wished at one time or another, myself included, that he could become a rock star. And Buddy is the perfect one to emulate: a poor, south Texas kid who becomes a major star, has a beautiful love affair, a fabulously solid marriage to a wonderful woman, then dies at the height of fame in a horrible accident. You don't even have to know who Buddy is to identify with that scenario.'

The production team were sincere in their desire to make a definitive motion picture about the early rock'n'roll era, and the fact that they have bent the facts slightly to suit their purpose can be excused when the result is in fact a very good movie. Their painstaking efforts are reflected in the care they took in the casting of the main characters. It had been agreed with Maria Elena that someone more or less unknown should be chosen for the title role so that emphasis would not be shifted away from Buddy onto a well-known celebrity. Further, it became crucial that the screen Holly and his two backing musicians would have to be reasonably accomplished musicians—the intention was that the music in the film should be recorded 'live', in order to preserve authenticity. As things transpired, the roles of the bass player and drummer were filled by actors who were not known musicians—although Charles Martin Smith, chosed for the part of Ray Bob, had appeared in several musical films previously, including *American Graffiti* and *Pat Garrett and Billy The Kid.* However, Smith had not taken on a directly musical role before, and the same was true of Don Stroud, who plays Jesse. Acting experience was on Stroud's side, however—he had appeared in over forty films and more than a hundred television shows, his film credits including *The Choirboys* and his TV credits *Petrocelli* and *Hawaii Five-O.* However, after dedicated practice before shooting began, Smith and Stroud carried off their roles as, respectively, upright bass player and drummer with little trouble.

But it was obvious from the start that the part which would have to be cast most carefully was that of Buddy Holly himself, and the final choice

Buddy and Maria contemplate the future in 'The Buddy Holly Story'.

was that of a little known, but still reasonably experienced actor/musician named Gary Busey. Busey was from Texas, which was obviously a good start, and after undergoing the make-up process, began to bear a remarkable likeness to Buddy Holly. But the crowning factor is Busey's voice—as soon as he begins to sing *Rock Around With Ollie Vee* in the roller skating rink, any doubts about his appearance disappear. For the duration of the movie, Busey *is* Buddy Holly.

In some ways Gary Busey's background was not dissimilar to Holly's. Like Holly, Busey acquired a guitar at an early age, and similarly, was more interested in music and acting, not to mention American football, than his traditional scholastic studies. To continue the parallels, Busey formed his first band—known as the Rubber Band—while still a student. The group was formed with three other students with Busey, as well as playing drums, being the group's main lyricist. The quartet played in public during the latter half of the sixties, eventually appearing in California at Disneyland, among many less notable venues. Near the end of their time together, the group changed its name to Carp—as Busey explained, 'We felt like trash fish. the joint we were playing was filled with bikers and junkies, and the bikers would roll their choppers in and shine their lights in our faces, and threaten to run 'em up onstage and kill us if we didn't play *Louie Louie* for thirty minutes.' As Carp, the group recorded an extremely obscure LP for Epic Records, which was titled after the name of the group. Listening to the album several years later, it's an acceptable, if unsensational record, bearing little resemblance to the music of Buddy Holly—rather, it's very much an early example of country rock, comprising a dozen 'story' songs. It's interesting to note that several of Busey's songs owe their lyrical inspiration to the gospel traditions of the Texas area—while Holly had a similar church background, he never used religious imagery in his songs, preferring to gain his inspiration from the maelstrom of boy/girl relationships.

The failure of Carp's LP seems to have been the final nail in the group's coffin, and not long after it was released, the group split up. Busey had by this time been introduced to the field of professional acting, working in initially minor roles in films and on television, and on the way becoming the last man to die in the TV Western series *Gunsmoke.* This was followed by an appearance in an episode of *The High Chapparal,* and by 1972, Busey had become reasonably well established as a 'bit-part' player on both TV programmes and in movies. 1972 was also the year when music began to creep back into his activities—a friend from Tulsa, Oklahoma, Gailard Sartain, asked Gary to appear on a local television show, which was seen by one of the city's more prominent musical personalities of the time, Leon Russell. Russell was impressed by Busey (who was appearing under the Sartain-inspired alias of Teddy Jack Eddy), and this led to Busey being invited to Russell's recording studio. (Sartain, by the way, plays the part of the Big Bopper in *The Buddy Holly Story.*) Russell eventually invited Busey to become part of his backing group, and under the alias of Teddy Jack Eddy, Busey has also appeared on several Leon Russell albums, including *Will O' The Wisp, Best of Leon, Make Love and Music* and *Wedding Album.* Involvement with Leon Russell was not Busey's only recording credit —again as Teddy Jack Eddy, he has also appeared on albums by the Nitty Gritty Dirt Band (*Dream*) and Kinky Friedman (*Lasso From El Paso*), while there are apparently plans afoot for a musical collaboration with country music superstar Willie Nelson, the idea being to produce a musical film based around Nelson's concept album, *Red Headed Stranger*.

It was during this time with Leon Russell that Busey began to appear in more films, including *The Last American Hero* (with Jeff Bridges), *Straight Time* (with Dustin Hoffmann), as Kris Kristofferson's road manager in the recent remake of *A Star Is Born,* and even more recently in the surfing movie, *Big Wednesday*. Since his triumphant appearance in *The Buddy Holly Story,* Gary Busey had managed to allow his film and musical careers to run parallel—Busey has his own group, the Teddy Jack Eddy Rendezvous—and at one point, there were even plans made for Busey and his celluloid sidekicks, Charles Martin Smith and Don Stroud, to tour America playing Buddy Holly songs. Busey's portrayal of Holly is masterly, indicating a great affection for his subject, and it seems that Gary Busey's future success as an actor is assured.

When the Buddy Holly film was first released in America, the critics were divided. The *Los Angeles Times* critic was full of praise of Busey's performance: 'For once there is no lip-synching to someone else's voice, no feigning with the fingers to somebody else's strumming. Busey does it all himself and it is one of those rare and stunning performances in which the person of the actor himself is totally lost to sight in his creation of someone else. The heart and soul and power of *The Buddy Holly Story* is the uncanny, marrow-deep, robust, exhilarating, likeable, superlative, overwhelmingly convincing portrayal by Gary Busey of the beanpole Texan who was one of the founding fathers of rock'n'roll in the mid-fifties.' This stands in contrast to the New York critic of *Melody Maker* who felt that 'it is sometimes disruptive to the flow of the biographical narrative to hear Busey sing (as it was for swing fans who groaned through James Stewart in *The Glenn Miller Story* doing Pennsylvania 65000 for a limpid eyed June Allyson) but overall the movie is entertaining and its intentions are nicely understated—and that lets you enjoy it'. The critics' general appreciation of Busey's performance was reflected in the Academy Award Nominations in 1979—Gary was one of five nominees for the coveted Oscar for Best Actor, alongside big star names like Jon Voight and Robert de Niro.

This concentration on Busey's performance to the exclusion of all other participants in the making of the film is hardly surprising, of course, although all the performances are excellent, but in particular the enormous experience and expertise supplied by Ed Cohen, Fred Bauer and Steve Rash should not be undervalued. Bauer, for instance, has spent

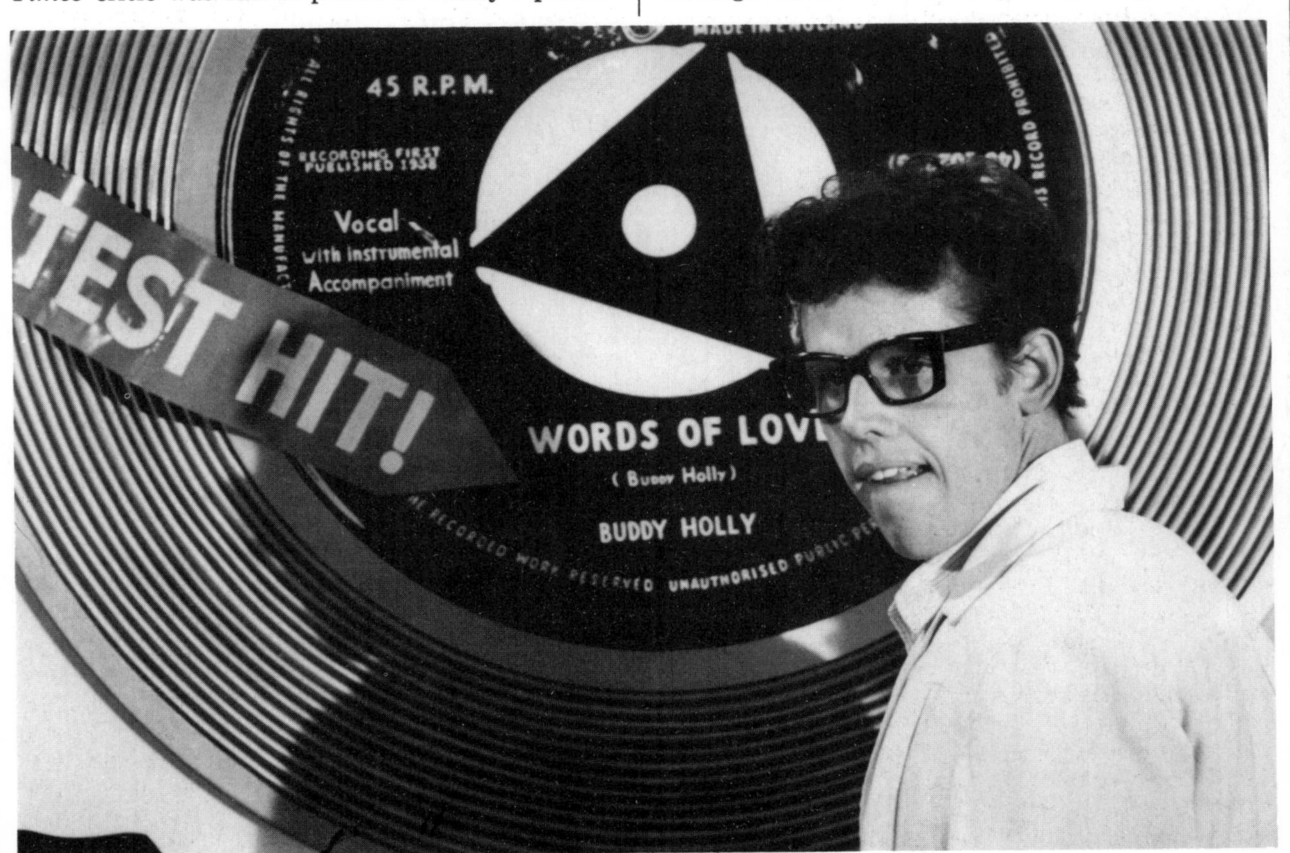

Gary Busey poses in front of a giant display copy of his single release in 'The Buddy Holly Story'.

nearly all his life in the world of entertainment, being the offspring of a vaudeville comic and a dancer. He studied radio and television at university, eventually working on both radio and TV stations in Pennsylvania, where his productions included documentaries, sport and entertainment. It was when Bauer met Steve Rash, who was directing a TV show titled *The Music Connection* which Bauer was producing, that the partnership was formed which eventually came up with *The Buddy Holly Story*. Although he is a TV director of long experience, the Buddy Holly film is Rash's first major screen credit. However, his credentials in the field of rock music on television are faultless, as he has worked on such successful shows as *The 20th Anniversary Of Rock'n'Roll, The Now Explosion, The Hitmakers* and *Rockin' In The U.S.A.* Several of these projects also involved Ed Cohen, whose tag of executive producer means that he is initially responsible for raising the finance required to make a film or television show. In this capacity, Cohen has allegedly become one of the largest sellers of motion pictures ideas to investment groups in the United States, having worked on films which featured stars like Donald Sutherland, Rod Taylor, Mickey Rooney and many others.

As a result, *The Buddy Holly Story* comes across as a professional production, even though it was made on a comparatively low budget—$2 million, as opposed to the $12 million spent on *Sergeant Pepper*. Bauer told *Buddy* magazine that he and his partners wanted to make 'an historic good-time movie about the roots of rock'n'roll. We chose Buddy Holly as our subject because he set the tone and established certain standards for the rock'n'roll idiom. He was the first to write, produce, sing and play his music all at once'. In Bauer's view Buddy was also the progenitor of a succession of white singers and instrumentalists who combined the black rhythm and blues sound with the more country white sound, and his life, which was untouched by scandal and drugs is one of the few that can be ethically glamourised. And it's undoubtedly true that the Bauer/Rash/Cohen combination has succeeded in one of its most laudable aims, to make a definitive movie tribute to rock'n'roll in general and Buddy's contribution to it in particular. Their expertise in presenting his music was deservedly recognised at the 1979 Academy Awards when the film won the Oscar for Original Score Adaptation.

In a radio interview, the producers were asked exactly why they had chosen the course of fictionalisation, and defended the numerous inaccuracies by saying that 'it made a better film'. They claimed in all fairness to be consciously creating a myth, by making *The Glenn Miller Story* of the seventies. Had they been able to include footage concerning Norman Petty's 'svengaliesque' patronage of Holly, perhaps the results would have been both more dramatic and substantially more accurate. As John Goldrosen commented, 'They could have told the truth and still been commercial.' But it is hard to see how the film-makers could literally 'tell the truth' without Norman Petty's co-operation. It is unfortunate that, as the Washington, DC, magazine *Unicorn Times* put it, 'Moviemakers have never been too successful with artists' lives, maybe because the drama of the creative process is often internal. *The Buddy Holly Story* fails in part by fabricating drama, and in that way distorting the real nature of Holly's career.'

There may be negative aspects to the film of *The Buddy Holly Story,* but with such an emotive subject it was obviously impossible to please everyone. In the end, any shortcomings should not be allowed to detract from the film's primary importance, both as an excellent motion picture in its own right, and also to give Holly's fellow Americans some idea of the heritage left by one of their number. As a direct result of the film, the residents of Lubbock have at last recognised the real importance of their youthful hero of twenty years ago. When Columbia Pictures decided to premiere the film in Lubbock, the city fathers agreed to name a park after him and The Buddy Holly Recreation Area was dedicated on May 18th, 1978 in the presence of Buddy's parents and brother Larry. There is no doubt that Buddy Holly was an enormous and original talent who until the release of *The Buddy Holly Story* had almost been forgotten by the majority of his compatriots. Perhaps now, with the release of *The Buddy Holly Story,* his genius will finally be accorded the place it deserves in the history of rock'n'roll.

Note: The records listed below are British and American releases by Buddy Holly with and without the Crickets. Due to the fact that Holly's recordings have been repackaged on several occasions, an element of duplication exists in many cases. Also, since the release of the six album boxed set, *The Complete Buddy Holly*, many earlier records have been deleted, and it is not possible to state with any degree of accuracy whether a particular item is readily available.

EXTENDED PLAY 7″ 45rpm RELEASES (EPs)
(Release dates from 1959 to 1965)

Label	U.S. Catalogue No. & Title
Decca	ED 2575—*That'll Be The Day* That'll Be The Day/Blue Day—Black Nights/ Ting-A-Ling/You Are My One Desire
Brunswick	EB 71036—*The Chirping Crickets* I'm Looking For Someone To Love/That'll Be The Day/Not Fade Away/Oh Boy.
Brunswick	EB 71038—*The Sound Of The Crickets* Maybe Baby/Rock Me My Baby/Send Me Some Lovin'/Tell Me How.
Coral	EC 81169—*Listen To Me* Listen To Me/Everyday/I'm Gonna Love You Too/ Peggy Sue.
Coral	EC 81182—*The Buddy Holly Story* Early In The Morning/Heartbeat/It Doesn't Matter Anymore/Raining In My Heart.
Coral	EC 81191—*Peggy Sue Got Married* Peggy Sue Got Married/Crying, Waiting, Hoping/ Learning The Game/That Makes It Tough.
Coral	EC 81193—*Brown Eyed Handsome Man* Brown Eyed Handsome Man/Bo Diddley/True Love Ways/Wishing.

Label	U.K. Catalogue No. & Title
Brunswick	OE 9456—*Buddy Holly No. 1* You Are My One Desire/Blue Days—Black Nights/ Modern Don Juan/Ting-A-Ling
Brunswick	OE 9457—*Buddy Holly No. 2* Girl On My Mind/Love Me/I'm Changing All Those Changes/Don't Come Back Knockin'
Coral	FEP 2002—*Buddy Holly*. Later titled *Listen To Me* Listen To Me/Peggy Sue/I'm Gonna Love You Too/ Everyday
Coral	FEP 2003—*The Sound Of The Crickets* Oh Boy/Not Fade Away/Maybe Baby/Tell Me How
Coral	FEP 2005—*Rave On* Rave On/Take Your Time/Early In The Morning/ Now We're One
Coral	FEP 2014—*It's So Easy* It's So Easy/Lonesome Tears/Think It Over/ Fool's Paradise
Coral	FEP 2015—*Heartbeat* Heartbeat/Well . . . All Right/Baby I Don't Care/ Little Baby
Coral	FEP 2032— *The Buddy Holly Story* It Doesn't Matter Anymore/Heartbeat/Raining In My Heart/Early In The Morning
Coral	FEP 2044—*The Late Great Buddy Holly* Look At Me/Ready Teddy/Mailman, Bring Me No More Blues/Words Of Love
Coral	FEP 2060—*Four More* Last Night/Send Me Some Lovin'/You've Got Love/ Rock Me My Baby
Coral	FEP 2062—*That'll Be The Day* That'll Be The Day/I'm Lookin' For Someone To Love/It's Too Late/An Empty Cup
Coral	FEP 2065—*Buddy—By Request* Brown Eyed Handsome Man/Slippin' And Slidin'/ Bo Diddley/Ummm, Oh Yeah
Coral	FEP 2066—*That Tex-Mex Sound* I'm Gonna Set My Foot Down/It's Not My Fault/ Rip It Up/Baby, Won't You Come Out Tonight
Coral	FEP 2067—*Wishing* Wishing/Reminiscing/Valley Of Tears/Learning The Game
Coral	FEP 2068—*Showcase No. 1* Honky Tonk/Gone/You're The One/I Guess I Was Just A Fool
Coral	FEP 2069—*Showcase No. 2* Blue Suede Shoes/Come Back Baby/Shake Rattle & Roll/Love's Made A Fool Of You
Coral	FEP 2070—*Buddy Holly Sings* Peggy Sue Got Married/Crying, Waiting, Hoping/ What To Do/That Makes It Tough

U.S. ALBUMS

Label	Catalogue No., Title & Release Date
Brunswick	54038—*The Chirping Crickets* November 1957 Oh Boy!/Not Fade Away/You've Got Love/Maybe Baby/It's Too Late/Tell Me How/That'll Be The Day/I'm Looking For Someone To Love/An Empty Cup/Send Me Some Lovin'/Rock Me My Baby. (Re-issued in 1962 as *Buddy Holly and The Crickets* on Coral 57405/757405)
Coral	57210—*Buddy Holly* March 1958 I'm Gonna Love You Too/Peggy Sue/Look At Me/ Listen To Me/Valley Of Tears/Ready Teddy/Every-day/Mailman, Bring Me No More Blues/Words Of Love/You're So Square/Rave On/Little Baby.
Decca	8707—*That'll Be The Day* April 1958 You Are My One Desire/Blue Days—Black Nights/ Modern Don Juan/Rock Around With Ollie Vee/ Ting-A-Ling/Girl On My Mind/That'll Be The Day/ Love Me/I'm Changing All Those Changes/Don't Come Back Knocking/Midnight Shift. (Re-issued in 1967 as *The Great Buddy Holly* on Vocalion 73811, with all tracks listed except 'Ting-A-Ling'. Subsequently re-numbered as MCA 20101 in the same form as the Vocalion release).
Coral	57279/75279—*The Buddy Holly Story* March 1959 Raining In My Heart/Early In The Morning/Peggy Sue/Maybe Baby/Everyday/Rave On/That'll Be The Day/Heartbeat/Think It Over/Oh Boy!/It's So Easy/It Doesn't Matter Anymore.
Coral	57326—*The Buddy Holly Story, Volume 2* March 1960 Peggy Sue Got Married/Well. . . All Right/What To Do/That Makes It Tough/Now We're One/Take Your Time/Crying, Waiting, Hoping/True Love Ways/Learning The Game/Little Baby/Moon-dreams/That's What They Say.
Coral	57426/757426—*Reminiscing* February 1963 Reminiscing/Slippin' And Slidin'/Bo Diddley/ Wait Till The Sun Shines, Nellie/Baby, Won't You Come Out Tonight/Brown Eyed Handsome Man/ Because I Love You/It's Not My Fault/I'm Gonna Set My Foot Down/Changing All Those Changes/ Rock-A-Bye-Rock.
Coral	57450/75450—*Showcase* May 1964 Shake, Rattle And Roll/Rock Around With Ollie Vee/ Honky Tonk/I Guess I Was Just A Fool/Ummm, Oh Yeah (Dearest)/You're The One/Blue Suede Shoes/ Come Back Baby/Rip It Up/Love's Made A Fool Of You/Gone/Girl On My Mind.
Coral	57463/757463—*Holly In The Hills* January 1965 I Wanna Play House With You/Door To My Heart/ Fool's Paradise/I Gambled My Heart/What To Do/ Wishing/Down The Line/Soft Place In My Heart/ Lonesome Tears/Gotta Get You Near Me Blues/ Flower Of My Heart/You And I Are Through.
Coral	CXB-8/7CXSB-8—*The Best of Buddy Holly* April 1966 Peggy Sue/Blue Suede Shoes/Learning The Game/ Brown Eyed Handsome Man/Everyday/Maybe Baby/Early In The Morning/Ready Teddy/It's Too Late/What To Do/Rave On/True Love Ways/It Doesn't Matter Anymore/Crying, Waiting, Hoping/ Moondreams/Rock Around With Ollie Vee/Raining In My Heart/Bo Diddley/That'll Be The Day/I'm Gonna Love You Too/Peggy Sue Got Married/ Shake, Rattle And Roll/That Makes It Tough/ Wishing.

Label	Catalogue No., Title & Release Date
Coral	757492—*Buddy Holly's Greatest Hits* March 1967 Peggy Sue/True Love Ways/Bo Diddley/What To Do/Learning The Game/It Doesn't Matter Anymore/That'll Be The Day/Oh Boy!/Early In The Morning/Brown Eyed Handsome Man/Everyday/Maybe Baby.
Coral	757504—*Giant* January 1969 Love Is Strange/Good Rockin' Tonight/Blue Monday/Have You Ever Been Lonely/Slippin' And Slidin'/You're The One/Dearest/Smokey Joe's Cafe/Ain't Got No Home/Holly Hop.
Vocalion	73923—*Good Rockin'* 1971 I Wanna Play House With You/Baby, I Don't Care/Little Baby/Ting-A-Ling/Take Your Time/Down The Line/Now We're One/Words of Love/That's What They Say/You And I Are Through.
Decca	DXSE7-207—*Buddy Holly: A Rock And Roll Collection* 1972 Rave On/Tell Me How/Peggy Sue Got Married/Slippin' And Slidin'/Oh Boy!/Not Fade Away/Bo Diddley/What To Do/Heartbeat/Well All Right/Words Of Love/Love's Made A Fool Of You/Reminiscing/Lonesome Tears/Listen To Me/Maybe Baby/Down The Line/That'll Be The Day/Peggy Sue/Brown Eyed Handsome Man/You're So Square/Crying, Waiting, Hoping/Ready Teddy/It Doesn't Matter Anymore. (Subsequently re-numbered as MCA 2-4009)
MCA	3040—*Buddy Holly/Crickets 20 Golden Greats* May 1978 That'll Be The Day/Peggy Sue/Words Of Love/Everyday/Not Fade Away/Oh Boy!/Maybe Baby/Listen To Me/Heartbeat/Think It Over/It Doesn't Matter Anymore/It's So Easy/Well All Right/Rave On/Raining In My Heart/True Love Ways/Peggy Sue Got Married/Bo Diddley/Brown Eyed Handsome Man/Wishing.

U.K. ALBUMS

Label	Catalogue No., Title & Release Date
Coral	LVA 9081—*The Chirping Crickets* March 1958 Oh Boy!/Not Fade Away/You've Got Love/Maybe Baby/It's Too Late/Tell Me How/That'll Be The Day/I'm Looking For Someone To Love/An Empty Cup/Send Me Some Lovin'/Last Night/Rock Me My Baby. (Re-issued in 1969 as Coral CP 20, and again in 1975 as Coral CDLM 8035)
Coral	LVA 9085—*Buddy Holly* July 1958 I'm Gonna Love You Too/Peggy Sue/Listen To Me/Look At Me/Valley Of Tears/Ready Teddy/Everyday/Mailman, Bring Me No More Blues/Words Of Love/(You're So Square) Baby I Don't Care/Rave On/Little Baby. (Re-issued in 1968 titled *Listen To Me* on MCA MUP/MUPS 312, and again in 1975 under its original title on Coral CDLM 8034)
Coral	LVA 9105—*The Buddy Holly Story* April 1959 Raining In My Heart/Early In The Morning/Peggy Sue/Maybe Baby/Everyday/Rave On/That'll Be The Day/Heartbeat/Think It Over/Oh Boy!/It's So Easy/It Doesn't Matter Anymore. (Re-issued in 1968 titled *Rave On*, MCA MUP/MUPS 313, and re-numbered in 1974 as MCA MCF 2614)
Coral	LVA 9127—*The Buddy Holly Story, Volume 2* November 1960 Peggy Sue Got Married/Well All Right/What To Do/That Makes It Tough/Now We're One/Take Your Time/Crying, Waiting, Hoping/True Love Ways/Learning The Game/Little Baby/Moondreams/That's What They Say. (Re-issued in 1968 titled *True Love Ways* on MCA MUP/MUPS 319)
Ace of Hearts	AH3—*That'll Be The Day* October 1961 You Are My One Desire/Blue Days—Black Nights/Modern Don Juan/Rock Around With Ollie Vee/Ting-A-Ling/Girl On My Mind/That'll Be The Day/Love Me/I'm Changing All Those Changes/Don't Come Back Knocking/Midnight Shift. (Re-issued in 1970 as Coral CP 24)
Coral	LVA 9212—*Reminiscing* April 1963 Reminiscing/Slippin' And Slidin'/Bo Diddley/Wait Till The Sun Shines, Nellie/Baby, Won't You Come Out Tonight/Brown Eyed Handsome Man/Because I Love You/It's Not My Fault/I'm Gonna Set My Foot Down/Changing All Those Changes/Rock A Bye Rock. (Re-issued in 1968 titled *Brown Eyed Handsome Man* on MCA MUP/MUPS 314, and re-numbered in 1974 as MCA MCF 2615)
Coral	LVA 9222—*Showcase* June 1964 Shake, Rattle And Roll/Rock Around With Ollie Vee/Honky Tonk/I Guess I Was Just A Fool/Ummm, Oh Yeah (Dearest)/You're The One/Blue Suede Shoes/Come Back Baby/Rip It Up/Love's Made A Fool Of You/Gone/Girl On My Mind. (Re-issued in 1968 titled *He's The One* on MCA MUP/MUPS 315)
Coral	LVA 9227—*Holly In The Hills* June 1965 I Wanna Play House With You/Door To My Heart/Baby, It's Love/I Gambled My Heart/Memories/Wishing/Down The Line/Soft Place In My Heart/Queen Of The Ballroom/Gotta Get You Near Me Blues/Flower Of My Heart/You And I Are Through. (Re-issued in 1968 titled *Wishing* on MCA MUP/MUPS 320)
Ace of Hearts	AH 148—*Buddy Holly's Greatest Hits* June 1967 Peggy Sue/That'll Be The Day/Listen To Me/Everyday/Oh Boy!/Not Fade Away/Maybe Baby/Rave On/Think It Over/It's So Easy/It Doesn't Matter Anymore/True Love Ways. (Re-issued in 1969 as Coral CP8, and in 1974 as Coral CDLM 8007, but in the latter case with two extra tracks, 'Raining In My Heart' and 'Peggy Sue Got Married').
Coral	CP/CPS 47—*Buddy Holly's Greatest Hits, Volume 2* May 1970 Early In The Morning/Well All Right/Heartbeat/Peggy Sue Got Married/What To Do/(You're So Square) Baby I Don't Care/ Words Of Love/Reminiscing/Brown Eyed Handsome Man/Bo Diddley/Wishing/Love's Made A Fool Of You.
MCA	MUPS 371—*Giant* February 1969 Love Is Strange/Good Rockin' Tonight/Blue Monday/Have You Ever Been Lonely/Slippin' And Slidin'/You're The One/Dearest/Smokey Joe's Cafe/Ain't Got No Home/Holly Hop.
Coral	CPS 71—*Remember* September 1971 Maybe Baby/That Makes It Tough/Crying, Waiting, Hoping/Lonesome Tears/That's My Desire/Real Wild Child/Peggy Sue Got Married/Fool's Paradise/Learning The Game/That's What They Say/Reminiscing/What To Do.
Coral	CDMSP 802—*Legend* October 1974 That'll Be The Day/I'm Looking For Someone To Love/Not Fade Away/Oh Boy!/Maybe Baby/Tell Me How/Think It Over/It's So Easy/Peggy Sue/Words Of Love/Everyday/I'm Gonna Love You Too/Listen To Me/Rave On/Well All Right/Heartbeat/Early In The Morning/Rock Around With Ollie Vee/Midnight Shift/Love's Made A Fool Of You/Wishing/Reminiscing/(You're So Square) Baby I Don't Care/Brown Eyed Handsome Man/Bo Diddley/It Doesn't Matter Anymore/Moondreams/True Love Ways/Raining In My Heart/Learning The Game/What To Do/Peggy Sue Got Married/Love Is Strange.
Music for Pleasure	MFP 50176—*Rave On* August 1975 Rave On/Love Me/It's Too Late/Take Your Time/That Makes It Tough/Gotta Get You Near Me Blues/

Label	Catalogue No., Title & Release Date
	Everyday/Baby Won't You Come Out Tonight/ Dearest/I'm Looking For Someone To Love/Now We're One/Holly Hop.
World Records	SM 301-5—*The Buddy Holly Story* November 1975 Rock Around With Ollie Vee/Blue Days, Black Nights/Baby Won't You Come Out Tonight/It's Not My Fault/Love Me/Girl On My Mind/That'll Be The Day/I'm Gonna Set My Foot Down/Ting-A-Ling/I'm Changing All Those Changes/Midnight Shift/Don't Come Back Knocking/You Are My One Desire/Modern Don Juan/I Guess I Was Just A Fool/Rock A Bye Rock/That'll Be The Day/I'm Looking For Someone To Love/Peggy Sue/Everyday/ Oh Boy!/Not Fade Away/Listen To Me/I'm Gonna Love You Too/Maybe Baby/Tell Me How/Rave On/Take Your Time/Think It Over/Fool's Paradise/ Early In The Morning/Now We're One/It's So Easy/ Lonesome Tears/Heartbeat/Well All Right/It Doesn't Matter Anymore/Raining In My Heart/ Peggy Sue Got Married/Crying, Waiting, Hoping/ True Love Ways/Learning The Game/What To Do/ Reminiscing/Brown Eyed Handsome Man/Bo Diddley/Wishing/Love's Made A Fool Of You/ Words Of Love/Moondreams/Love Is Strange/ You've Got Love/Dearest/Send Me Some Lovin'/ Because I Love You/Look At Me/Rock Me My Baby/It's Too Late/You're The One/Valley Of Tears/Little Baby/Come Back Baby/Last Night/ That's What They Say/Ready Teddy/Baby I Don't Care/Slippin' And Slidin'/Blue Suede Shoes/Shake Rattle And Roll/Rip It Up/Ain't Got No Home/ Honky Tonk/Maybe Baby/An Empty Cup/Wait Till The Sun Shines, Nellie/Slippin' And Slidin'/ Mailman Bring Me No More Blues/That's My Desire/That Makes It Tough/Holly Hop.
Coral	CDLM 8038—*The Nashville Sessions* November 1975 You Are My One Desire/Blue Days—Black Nights/ Modern Don Juan/Rock Around With Ollie Vee/ Ting-A-Ling/Girl On My Mind/That'll Be The Day/ Love Me/I'm Changing All Those Changes/Don't Come Back Knockin'/Midnight Shift/Rock Around With Ollie Vee.
Coral	CDLM 8055—*Western and Bop* November 1977 Gotta Get You Near Me Blues/Soft Place In My Heart/Flower Of My Heart/Baby It's Love/ Memories/Door To My Heart/Queen Of The Ballroom/You And I Are Through/Down The Line/ Maybe Baby/Gone/Because I Love You/It's Not My Fault/I Guess I Was Just A Fool/I Gambled My Heart/Have You Ever Been Lonely.
MCA	EMTV 8—*Buddy Holly Lives—Buddy Holly & The Crickets 20 Golden Greats* February 1978 That'll Be The Day/Peggy Sue/Words Of Love/ Everyday/Not Fade Away/Oh Boy!/Maybe Baby/ Listen To Me/Heartbeat/Think It Over/It Doesn't Matter Anymore/It's So Easy/Well All Right/Rave On/Raining In My Heart/True Love Ways/Peggy Sue Got Married/Bo Diddley/Brown Eyed Handsome Man/Wishing.
Coral	CDMSP 807—*The Complete Buddy Holly* March 1979 Gotta Get You Near Me Blues/Soft Place In My Heart/Door To My Heart/Flower Of My Heart/ Baby It's Love/Memories/Queen Of The Ballroom/ I Gambled My Heart/You And I Are Through/ Gone/Have You Ever Been Lonely/Down The Line/ Brown Eyed Handsome Man/Bo Diddley/Good Rockin' Tonight/Rip It Up/Blue Monday/Honky Tonk/Blue Suede Shoes/Shake Rattle & Roll/Ain't Got No Home/Holly Hop/Baby Let's Play House/ I'm Gonna Set My Foot Down/Baby Won't You Come Out Tonight/Changing All Those Changes/ Rock-a-Bye Rock/It's Not My Fault/I Guess I Was Just A Fool/Love Me/Don't Come Back Knockin'/ Midnight Shift/Blue Days—Black Nights/Rock Around With Ollie Vee/I'm Changing All Those Changes/That'll Be The Day/Girl On My Mind/ Ting-A-Ling/Because I Love You/Rock Around With Ollie Vee/Modern Don Juan/You Are My One Desire/That'll Be The Day/I'm Looking For Someone To Love/Last Night/Maybe Baby/Words Of Love/Peggy Sue/Everyday/Mailman, Bring Me No More Blues/Listen To Me/I'm Gonna Love You Too/Not Fade Away/Ready Teddy/Oh Boy/Tell Me How/Maybe Baby/Send Me Some Lovin'/Little Baby/Take Your Time/Rave On/You've Got Love/ Valley Of Tears/Rock Me My Baby/Baby I Don't Care/It's Too Late/An Empty Cup/Look At Me/Think It Over/Fools Paradise/Early In The Morning/Now We're One/Lonesome Tears/Heartbeat/It's So Easy/Well All Right/Love's Made A Fool Of You/Wishing/Reminiscing/Come Back Baby/That's My Desire/True Love Ways/Moondreams/Raining In My Heart/It Doesn't Matter Anymore/Peggy Sue Got Married/Crying, Waiting, Hoping/Learning The Game/That Makes It Tough/What To Do/That's What They Say/Wait Till The Sun Shines Nellie/Ummm, Oh Yeah (Dearest)/Smokey Joe's Cafe/Slippin' And Slidin'/ Love Is Strange/Slippin' And Slidin'/Learning The Game/Crying, Waiting, Hoping/What To Do/That Makes It Tough/Peggy Sue Got Married/That's What They Say/Dearest/You're The One/Slippin' And Slidin'/Dearest/Love Is Strange/Peggy Sue Got Married/That Makes It Tough/Learning The Game/You're The One/Real Wild Child/Oh You Beautiful Doll/Jole Blon/When Sin Stops/Stay Close To Me/Don't Cha Know/Interview in Topeka, Kansas/Ed Sullivan Show—That'll Be The Day/ Peggy Sue/Interview with Ed Sullivan/Interview with Alan Freed/Interview with Dick Clark.

U.S. SINGLES

Label	Catalogue No. & Title		Year of Release
Decca	29854	Blue Days, Black Nights/ Love Me	1956
Decca	30166	Modern Don Juan/ You Are My One Desire	1956
Brunswick	55009	That'll Be The Day/ I'm Looking For Someone To Love	1957
Coral	61852	Words Of Love/Mailman, Bring Me No More Blues	1957
Decca	30434	Rock Around With Ollie Vee/ That'll Be The Day	1957
Coral	61885	Peggy Sue/Everyday	1957
Brunswick	55035	Oh Boy!/Not Fade Away	1957
Decca	30543	Love Me/ You Are My One Desire	1958
Coral	61947	I'm Gonna Love You Too/ Listen To Me	1958
Brunswick	55053	Maybe Baby/Tell Me How	1958
Coral	61985	Rave On/Take Your Time	1958
Brunswick	55072	Think It Over/Fool's Paradise	1958
Decca	30650	Girl On My Mind/Ting-A-Ling	1958
Coral	62006	Early In The Morning/ Now We're One	1958
Brunswick	55094	It's So Easy/Lonesome Tears	1958
Coral	62017	Real Wild Child/Oh You Beautiful Doll—by 'Ivan'	1958
Coral	62051	Heartbeat/Well All Right	1958
Coral	62074	It Doesn't Matter Anymore/ Raining In My Heart	1959
Coral	62134	Peggy Sue Got Married/ Crying, Waiting, Hoping	1959
Coral	62210	True Love Ways/ That Makes It Tough	1960
Coral	62329	Reminiscing/Wait Till The Sun Shines, Nellie	1962
Coral	62352	Bo Diddley/True Love Ways	1963
Coral	62369	Brown Eyed Handsome Man/ Wishing	1963
Coral	62390	Rock Around With Ollie Vee/ I'm Gonna Love You Too	1964
Coral	62407	Maybe Baby/Not Fade Away	1964
Coral	62448	What To Do/ Slippin' And Slidin'	1965
Coral	62554	Rave On/Early In The Morning	1968
Coral	62558	Love Is Strange/You're The One	1969
Coral	65618	That'll Be The Day/I'm Looking For Someone To Love	1972
MCA	60000	That'll Be The Day/I'm Looking For Someone To Love	1973
MCA	60004	Peggy Sue/Everyday	1973
MCA	40905	It Doesn't Matter Anymore/ Peggy Sue	1978

U.K. SINGLES

Label	Catalogue No. & Title		Year of Release
Brunswick	O 5581	Blue Days, Black Nights/ Love Me	1956
Coral	Q 72279	That'll Be The Day/I'm Looking For Someone To Love	1957
Coral	Q 72293	Peggy Sue/Everyday	1957
Coral	Q 72298	Oh Boy/Not Fade Away	1957
Coral	Q 72288	Listen To Me/I'm Gonna Love You Too	1958
Coral	Q 72307	Maybe Baby/Tell Me How	1958
Coral	Q 72325	Rave On/Take Your Time	1958
Coral	Q 72329	Think It Over/Fool's Paradise	1958
Coral	Q 72333	Early In The Morning/ Now We're One	1958
Coral	Q 72341	Real Wild Child/Oh You Beautiful Doll—by 'Ivan'	1958
Coral	Q 72345	It's So Easy/Lonesome Tears	1958
Coral	Q 72346	Heartbeat/Well All Right	1958
Coral	Q 72360	It Doesn't Matter Anymore/ Raining In My Heart	1959
Brunswick	O 5800	Midnight Shift/Rock Around With Ollie Vee	1959
Coral	Q 72376	Peggy Sue Got Married/ Crying, Waiting, Hoping	1959
Coral	Q 72392	Heartbeat/Everyday	1960
Coral	Q 72397	True Love Ways/Moondreams	1960
Coral	Q 72411	Learning The Game/ That Makes It Tough	1960
Coral	Q 72419	What To Do/ That's What They Say	1961
Coral	Q 72432	(You're So Square) Baby I Don't Care/Valley Of Tears	1961
Coral	Q 72445	Look At Me/Mailman, Bring Me No More Blues	1961
Coral	Q 72449	Listen To Me/Words Of Love	1962
Coral	Q 72455	Reminiscing/Wait Till The Sun Shines, Nellie	1962
Coral	Q 72459	Brown Eyed Handsome Man/ Slippin' And Slidin'	1963
Coral	Q 72463	Bo Diddley/It's Not My Fault	1963
Coral	Q 72466	Wishing/Because I Love You	1963
Coral	Q 72469	What To Do/ Ummm, Oh Yeah (Dearest)	1963
Coral	Q 72472	You've Got Love/ An Empty Cup	1964
Coral	Q 72475	Love's Made A Fool Of You/ You're The One	1964
Coral	Q 72483	Maybe Baby/That's My Desire	1966
MCA	MU 1012	Peggy Sue/Rave On	1968
MCA	MU 1017	Oh Boy!/That'll Be The Day	1968
MCA	MU 1059	Love Is Strange/You're The One	1969
MCA	MU 1081	It Doesn't Matter Anymore/ Maybe Baby	1969
MCA	MU 1116	Rave On/Ummm, Oh Yeah (Dearest)	1970
MCA	MMU 1198	That'll Be The Day/ Well All Right/Everyday	1973
MCA	MCA 119	It Doesn't Matter Anymore/ True Love Ways/Brown Eyed Handsome Man	1974
MCA	MCA 207	Oh Boy!/Everyday	1975
MCA	MCA 252	True Love Ways/It Doesn't Matter Anymore/Raining In My Heart/Moondreams	1976
MCA	MCA 253	Peggy Sue/Rave On/Rock Around With Ollie Vee/ Midnight Shift	1976
MCA	MCA 254	Maybe Baby/Think It Over/ That'll Be The Day/It's So Easy	1976
MCA	MCA 344	Wishing/Love's Made A Fool Of You	1978

ACKNOWLEDGEMENTS

If you find this book enjoyable, I'd like you to know that a good deal of the information it contains was provided by a small army of interested individuals who were kind enough to talk to me and, knowingly or unknowingly, supply material which has been incorporated in the text or illustrations. Special thanks are due to John Beecher for supplying photographs from his collection, also Flair Photography, Dezo Hoffman and MCA; and Stuart Grundy, Peter O'Brien and Richard Wootton, who particularly put themselves out for this enterprise, while credit is due to the following periodicals for their invaluable groundwork: *Buddy, Club Sandwich, Country Music People, Crawdaddy, Deja Vu, Melody Maker, Omaha Rainbow, Picking Up The Tempo, Rolling Stone, Trouser Press, Unicorn Times, Zigzag*.

To this list should be added the following names, whose words, whether written or spoken, are either incorporated or were considered for inclusion: Malcolm Jones, Martin B., Chet Flippo, Ben Fong-Torres, Pete Frame, Steve Frampton, Paul Gambaccini, Willy Glass, Charlie Gillett, Stuart Coleman, John Goldrosen, Kingsley Grimble, Brandon Harris, Rob Kelly, Dave Laing, Barry Lazell, Dick Middleton, Stanley Mieses, Tom Miller, Trudy Patterson, Tony Brainsby, Bert Muirhead, Geoff Thorn, Keith Smith, Rocky Prior, Joe Sasfy, Bix Palmer and Stephen Peebles. To all the above, and especially to Nicky, Sandra and Terry of Plexus, my grateful thanks, and my apologies to anyone who feels he or she has been forgotten. It has not been possible in all cases to trace the copyright sources, and we would be glad to hear from any such unacknowledged copyright holders.

The film *The Buddy Holly Story* is an Innovisions-ECA Production, and is distributed in the United Kingdom by *Entertainment Film Distributors*.

John Tobler
May 1979.